First published in May 2013 by Jay Gravelle, Everett, WA 98201

First Printing – May 2013
Second Printing – July 2013

IBSN: 978-1-937358-25-9

Disclaimer:

You are urged to use this book for informational purposes only and to seek regular training with a qualified instructor.

Karate is physically demanding and can be dangerous if done improperly. We cannot accept any responsibility for accident or injury caused through misinterpretation or misuse of its contents. As a martial art and semi-contact sport, minor injuries (such as bruising or blisters) are inevitable and participants may expect to receive them from time to time in the course of normal training. As with any program of strenuous exercise, it is recommended that a person with any existing injury/illness, or any doubt as to the risks, should consult their physician/doctor for advice before commencing training.

The NorthWest Budokan Karate is committed to maintaining an extremely high level of training and the welfare of its members is of concern; however the responsibility falls on the individual member to know their own limitations and to practice Karate responsibly.

Members are obliged to report any existing/new injuries and illnesses to the Sensei prior to training. Whilst NorthWest Budokan Karate and its instructors will ensure that all reasonable precautions to minimize the potential for injury are taken, they cannot be held liable for personal injury sustained by any member during training or competition.

Acknowledgments

Dedicated to my friend, my partner and my wife, Bernadette. Without her encouragement this book would not have been written and in fact a lot of my karate would not be what it is today. She gives me constant encouragement in karate and life.

To Master Fusei Kise, Kaicho Isao Kise and all of my senseis. Without your instruction I would never know the joys of the martial arts.

To all of my students, thank you for challenging me and being a part of my karate, the NorthWest Budokan and OSMKKF (Okinawa Shorin-Ryu Matsumura Seito Karate and Kobudo Federation).

I want to thank my students for the time and energy that was spent posing for all the pictures. You all helped with your contribution.

Thank you one and all.

Shihan Jay Gravelle
NorthWest Budokan

Cover photo of Master Kise and Kyoshi Jay Gravelle taken by Bernadette.

PREFACE:

I've been asked, "Why do we have to learn so many different tuite/self-defense techniques for the same grab"? Although one may find a "favorite" technique for a grab, keep in mind that everyone is different and what works for one person may not work for another. This is due to age, height, weight, strength, flexibility, pain tolerance and a variety of other circumstances. To be able to pass on information to others you must learn all the different techniques to not only find what works best for you, but what may work best for someone else. As I've said many times, "There's no magic in karate, it's just body physics." Body physics are different for everyone.

There are many nuances and subtle moves that cannot be shown in a book. This book is meant as a reference for tuite and *not* as an initial learning manual. You are urged to use this book for informational purposes only and to seek regular training with a qualified instructor. I have included a place for notes on almost every page and encourage everyone to make their own notes during and after each tuite session.

While I have taken every effort to the accuracy of content and data in this book, techniques in this book are all subject to change. Updates will always occur. This information is a compilation of seminars from Master Kise and Kaicho as well as many seminars I've attended over the years.

In the past I tried to tweak a technique, thinking it would improve the technique. After asking Master Kise if it was better, he would show me why it didn't work and why the original technique works the best. Because of his teachings I have tried my best to maintain his techniques.

Please be careful when practicing tuite. When practicing with a partner be aware of their reactions and stop when you see any indication of pain. The universal sign to stop is when your *partner* slaps himself or you, indicating they are in pain.

Respect of your partner is very important and must be understood. Bow to your partner before and after to show this respect to each other.

Although the techniques are shown in the pictures as one side of the body, remember to practice all the techniques using both sides. Practice the tuite that gives you the most challenge more often than the simple ones.

With tuite you'll find sometimes an opponent resists or is able to slip out of a lock. In "real life" situations this will occur and it will help you to work on drills that will help you go from one lock to another lock. I encourage everyone to experiment and practice with these.

Tuite is not about brute strength, but about technique. One place where strength is very important is your fingers. Strengthen your hands and fingers. This will help with your grip and when you hit pressure points. Your grip is needed to add to tuite techniques by twisting or tearing.

Tuite: "It's all about body physics!"

Table of Contents

Chapter 1 - What is Tuite?

Tui means "to grab" and 'Te' means "hand", so the literal translation of tuite means to grab an opponent using the hands. Tuite is self-defense and sometimes much more. It can be as simple as an escape or as complex and devastating as a bone breaking takedown.

Tuite is an old art of Okinawa and was primarily limited to Royal families, their bodyguards and the privileged few. Although tuite is an Okinawan martial art, the Okinawan people were quite seafaring and many of them made trips to China where they may have studied Chin na. Although Chin na may be some of the roots of tuite, tuite is not Chin na and should not be confused with it. Just as karate has its roots in kung fu, it is not kung fu.

Tuite involves grabbing, joint manipulation, pressure points, grappling, striking, kicks, tearing, control, throws and balance. There are times when you might want to control an opponent rather than hurting them with a strike and a joint lock would be a much better response. The joints within the body move many different ways and knowing which way they *don't* move and how to apply the pressure will control your opponent.

Grappling is not the way of a karateka, but there are times when you might be grabbed and tuite is the grappling moves for those times. Ideally you want to stay upright and be able to move quickly, being aware of a second or third attacker, but there's always the chance of being taken to the ground. Although tuite is practiced while standing upright, the techniques can also be applied when you're on the ground. This is very important to realize, as the joints and pressure points still work while you're on the ground.

Tuite isn't about strength. It's about body physics. I've seen younger and smaller girls and women who have brought down much larger men and have them ask for mercy. It doesn't matter how big or strong you are, if your joint is being pushed in the way it isn't meant to bend, it *will* hurt and you *will* follow or the joint *will* break. This is all about body physics.

Knowing the body's range of motion and weaknesses are key to using tuite. To understand *how* tuite works, one should study the human anatomy and get knowledge of the skeletal joints, muscles and tendons and the weaknesses of each.

The limits of the physical movement and pressure on joints, tendons, ligaments and nerves allow you to exploit the weaknesses. Pressure points in tuite help to short circuit the nerves to weaken the parts of the body and assist with the mechanical aspect of tuite. Twisting the wrist beyond the limits of motion will control the attacker. Striking a pressure point at the same time will assist in weakening the wrist and allow you to control the joint with less effort. Tuite is more about control than dislocating the joints.

It is true when practicing with a partner, who knows what you're doing, might be able to resist to a point, but the real truth is the more they resist, the easier it is to really hurt them. Even if one technique doesn't work, a simple change to another technique will prove to them it does work and in the process inflict more pain than they expected.

Tuite is not meant to be an offensive martial art and is primarily for defense to a grab. Ideally a karateka doesn't want to be grabbed, but the reality is there is always that chance and it's best to be prepared for anything that may happen in a confrontation.

Tuite is one of three parts of the OSMKKF. The other two being empty hand "Karate" and weapons or "Kobudo".

Tuite is an integral part of our system of karate and is intertwined in many aspects of kata and other techniques.

Chapter 2 - Body Physics

To understand tuite it is very important to know something about body physics, as to how certain joints bend or do not bend and how they function mechanically. Tuite is primarily used against the finger, wrist, elbow and shoulder joints. *These joints can only be extended so far.* All the joints can be dislocated when force is applied beyond the limits of each joint.

To better understand the biomechanics of the joints it is important to understand how they bend. The joints are dependent on the muscles, ligaments, tendons and bones. Extending the joints beyond their normal ranges (physiologic barrier) causes pain and is key to many of the tuite techniques. Extending the joints even farther (anatomical barrier) will cause dislocation or breaks.

Without going into the scientific anatomy of the joints, the following explains some very basics of the joints. The ranges of motion for the joints are different between individuals. Some people are very flexible and some are very stiff. As a rule, youth are much more flexible than adults and women are slightly more flexible them men.

The following information is to illustrate the ranges of the joints in the many ways we bend each of them in tuite. There are many publications that go much farther into detail and I encourage everyone to research the human anatomy in order to help with tuite and understand the elements of the joints and how they work.

Shoulder joint

The shoulder joint is a ball and socket joint and has the following normal ranges of movement: Flexion, Extension, Adduction, Abduction and Medial Rotation.

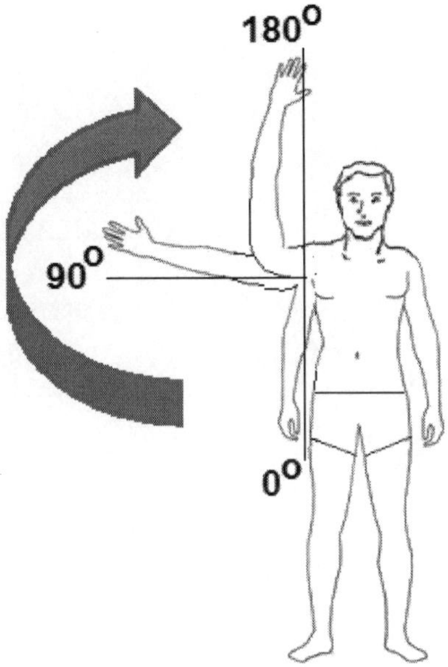

Shoulder abduction

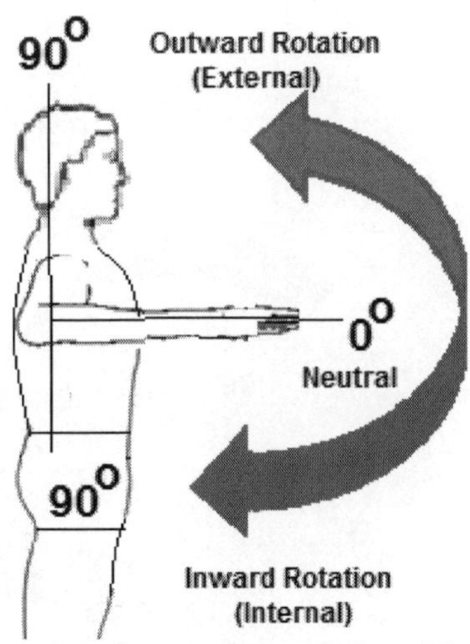

Internal and external rotation of shoulder at 90 degrees

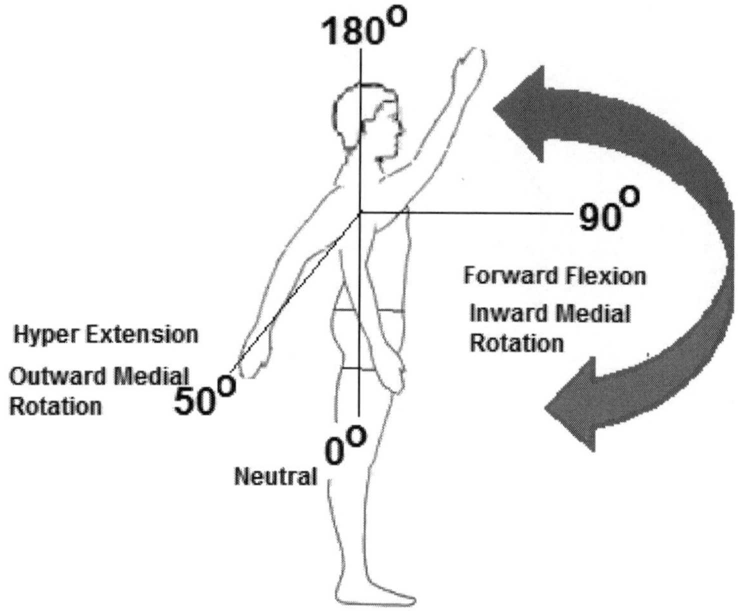

Forward rotation of shoulder

Elbow

The elbow is known as a hinge joint, but is actually three joints. Normal elbow flexion varies between 135 degrees to 155 degrees.

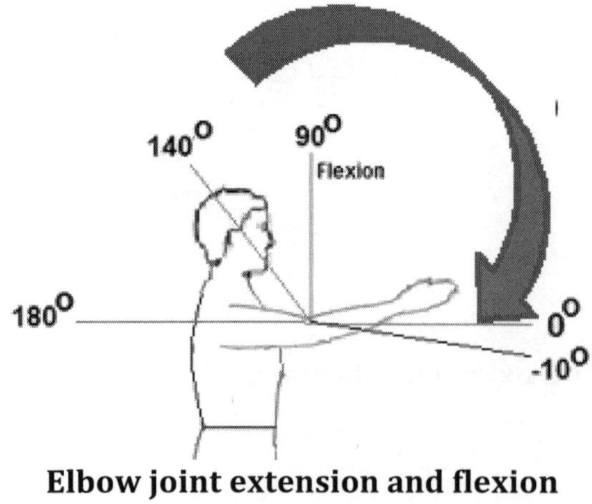

Elbow joint extension and flexion

Wrist

The wrist joint is made up of several joints and these are the approximate ranges of motion for the average adult wrist.

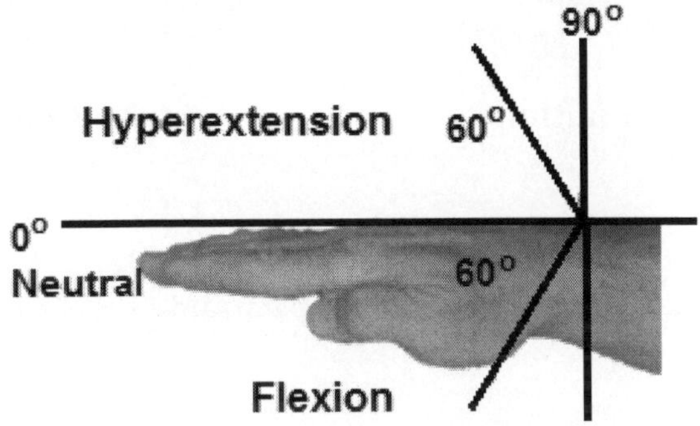

Wrist flexion and extension

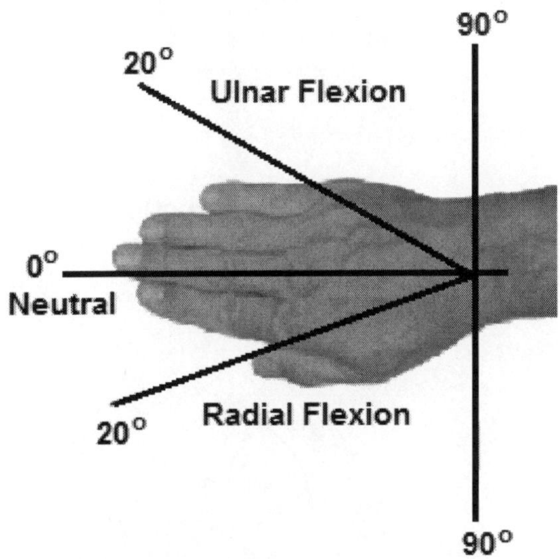

Wrist radial and ulnar flexion

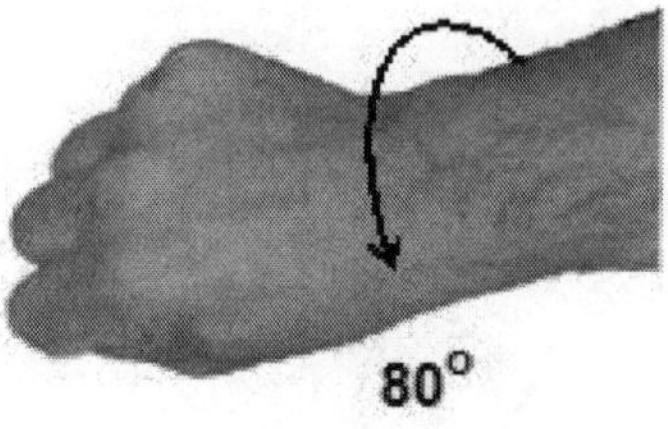

Pronation

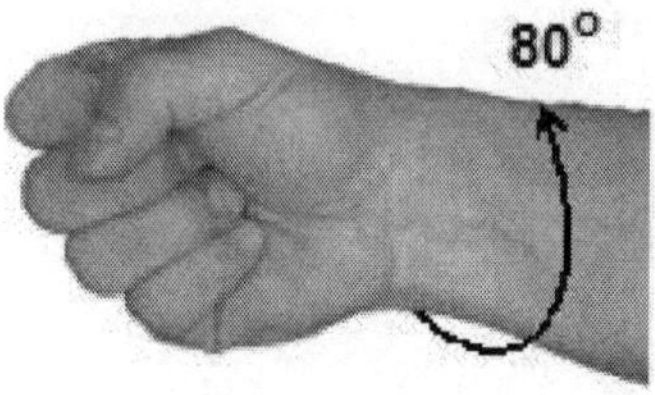

Supination

Hand

The hand has 19 bones with 5 in the palm and 14 in the fingers.

Fingers

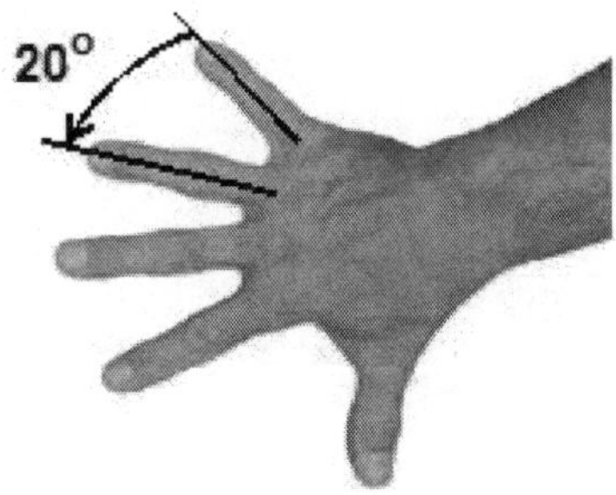

Normal MCP Adduction

Thumb

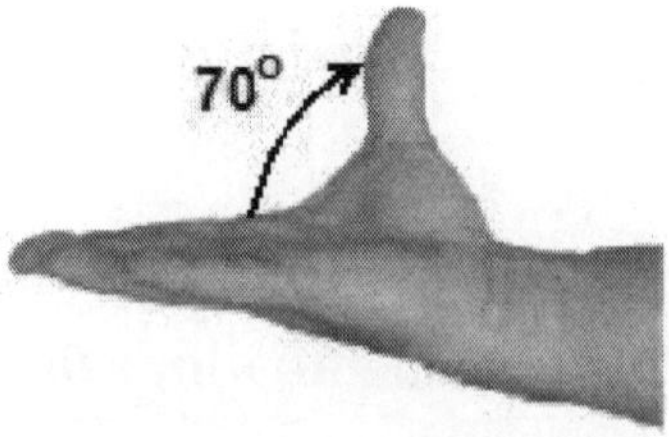

Normal CMC abduction

Fulcrums and how they're used in Tuite

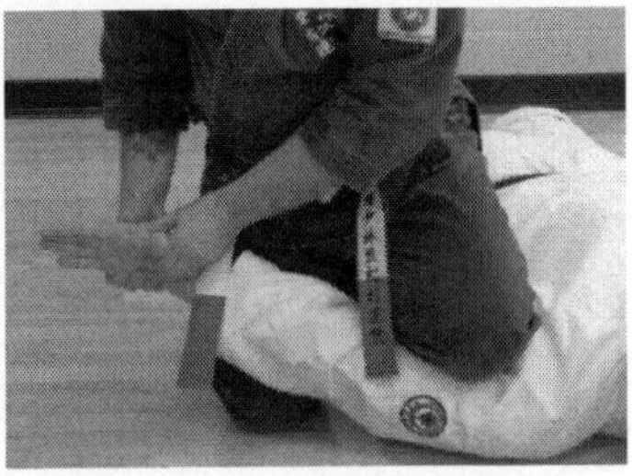

Fulcrums are a point or base that's used to hyperextend a joint thus, causing additional pain. An arm bar is an excellent example of using a fulcrum.

In this picture the defender's knee is the fulcrum.

Balance and Positioning

Balance and positioning are important to having the advantage and keeping the opponent at a disadvantage.

Keep your balance solid, firm and upright. Being balanced is an advantage for you. Being off balanced is an advantage for your attacker.

Never bow to your attacker, make your attacker bow to you. When you bow it releases the pressure on your opponent, but when you stay upright it is your opponent who will feel the pressure. A lot of people try to put more force on a lock and feel they have to bend over to do so. ***Do not bend over!***

To help you with this concept, think of the proud samurai of old Okinawa. In being very proud, they never bowed to anyone inferior to them, but expected everyone to bow to them. This was a position of strength and power. Staying proud and upright will strengthen your tuite.

Position yourself where you are the strongest and your opponent is the weakest. Angle your body position by using change body, but keep your stance very solid with both feet planted firmly on the ground. If you find yourself too far away, slide into your attacker, but do not reach for them.

Keep your hands close to your body, as tuite is not about strength, but about angles, grip and position.

Meridians and Nervous System

Going into meridians would be a book by itself and there is a complete eastern science around them. Western medicine tends to equate meridians with nerve pathways. Looking at the layout of meridians and the nervous system would support this. Meridians are used in several other studies such as acupuncture, reiki massage and

Shiatsu. Meridians or nerves are energy lines that traverse the body and affect other systems within the body. Hitting pressure points can interrupt the energy flow of the body. Blocking the flow of energy can assist in your tuite techniques. Although this book will not go into meridians or the nervous system, the study of these along with pressure points are recommended to advance your tuite techniques. Many sources are available.

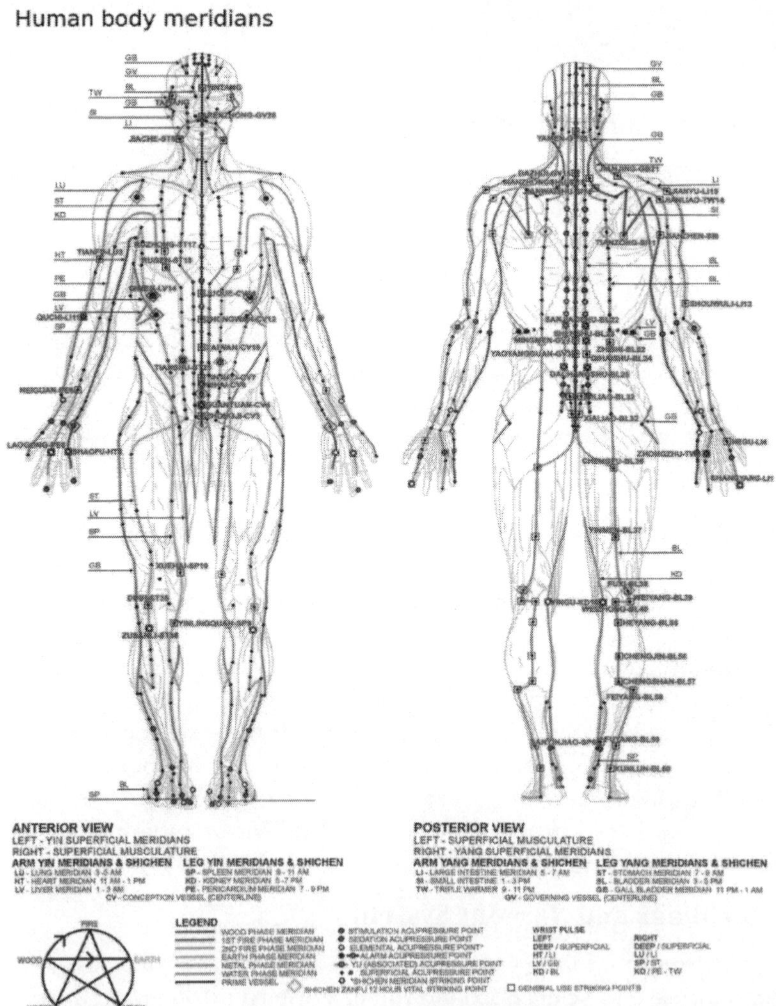

Permission was given for the use of the image at Wikimedia Commons

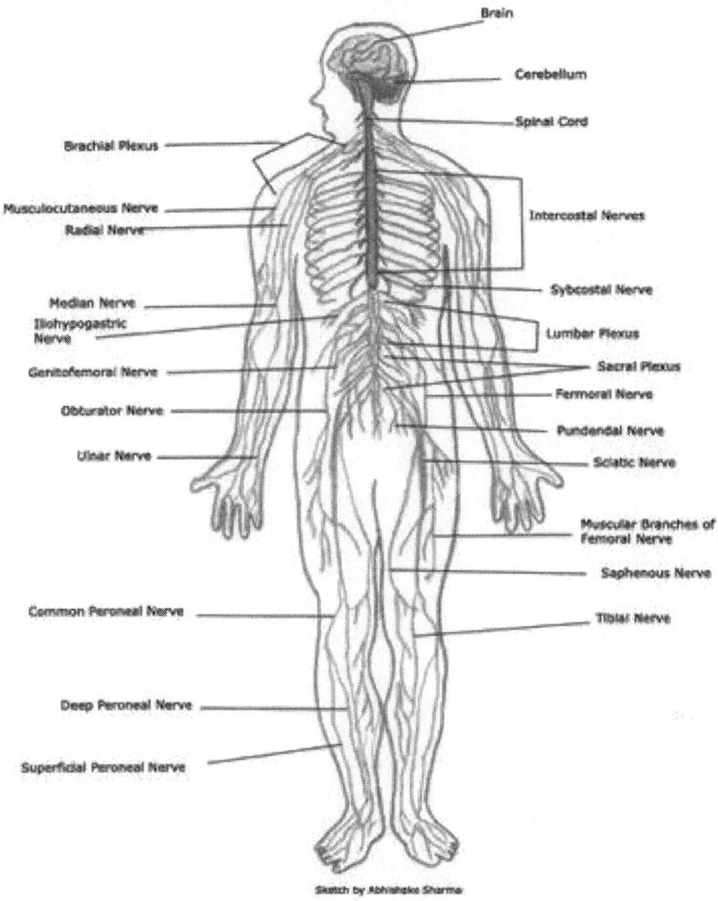

Nervous System Diagram

Permission was given for the use of the image at Wikimedia Commons

Chapter 3 – Tuite Application in Kata

> ***"Question:*** *When is a block not really a block?*
> ***Answer:*** *When it could be tuite."*

Tuite is an integral part of OSMKKF and is intertwined in many aspects of kata and other techniques.

The *bunkai* (the personal interpretations of each move) of kata will open up your eyes in the use of tuite within kata. One of the biggest moves showing the use of tuite is in any of the katas where you have a 270 degree turn such as in the kata *Pinan Shodan.* The next move after the spear hand strike is a 270 degree turn. Now ask yourself why would you do a 270 degree turn to do a down block when a simple 45 degree turn in the opposite direction would be faster? Think tuite… Picture this as someone grabbing your arm. For the 270 degree turn, picture the use of a wrist out turn as you do the turn.

Another simple use of tuite in kata is the box chamber. Used in several katas, picture being grabbed and then pulling the attacker into a lock to the box chamber.

Researching the bunkai of kata will open up many uses of tuite within our katas. In looking at bunkai don't just follow the kata, but use the kata moves as a starting point to examine all the possible uses of each move. There is not any wrong bunkai.

In karate we look at the bunkai for kata. When you look for tuite within the kata bunkai, you will find a vast, hidden treasure chest of techniques. This is to say tuite isn't the only bunkai, but one possible aspect of the kata bunkai. The techniques can be as simple as an escape or a complex take down. The important thing is to ***"think outside the kata box".***

In many systems' kihon (basic) katas, there are techniques that will have the karateka move 270 degrees in one direction. In Fu Kyu Gata Kata Ichi on the eighth move there is a punch with the ninth move being a 270 degree turn to a down block.

As a beginner, when one first learns the kata, the move makes sense. After all a down block is to defend against an attacker's kick. The question you need to ask is why would someone do a 270 degree turn when a simple 45 degree turn in the other direction would be quicker?

The answer comes down to tuite. Let's take another look at the 270 degree turn that makes a little bit more sense. This picture shows redirecting the attacker after the punch on the eighth move. To use tuite for the ninth move, grab the attacker's hand and use a wrist out turn while doing the 270 degree turn. Throw the attacker to the ground and this will leave you in the same position as when you did a down block.

Using Tuite in Kata – 270 degree turn with a Single Attacker.

Fig. 1 – Fu Kyu Gata Kata Ichi 8th move – middle punch.

Fig. 2 – Attacker grabs the punching arm.

Fig. 3 – Starting the 9th move, grab the top of the attacker's hand with your free hand.

Fig. 4 –Roll your grabbed hand over and grab the attacker's hand with both of your hands.

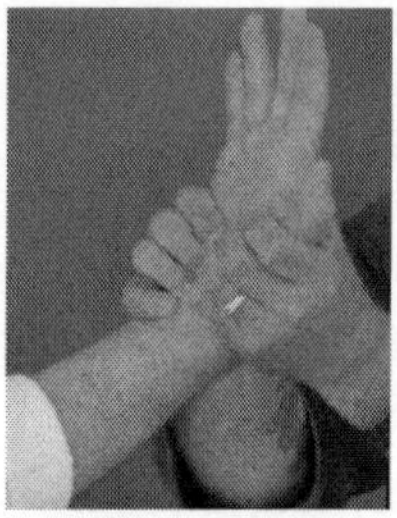

Fig. 5 – Detail of the attacker's hand being grabbed.

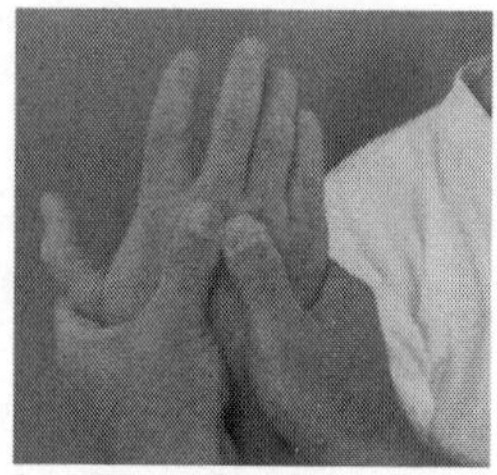

Fig. 6 – Detail of the back side of the attacker's hand being grabbed.

Fig. 7 – Stepping back and starting the 270 degree turn, bring the attacker down.

Fig. 8 –Finish the 9th move with a wrist lock.

Using Tuite in Kata – 270 degree Turn with Two Attackers

Another bunkai on this would be against two attackers and throwing the first attacker into the second attacker. Follow the same start of the technique in the first example, but instead of throwing the attacker to the ground the attacker is thrown into the second attacker.

Fig. 9 – 8th move, two attackers.

Fig. 10 –Grab the attacker as in the same fig. 3 – fig. 6.

Fig. 11 – Step back and throw the first attacker into the second attacker.	Fig. 12 –Finish with bringing both attackers to the ground.

Kata is one way to practice your karate without a partner. However, doing the moves without understanding the purpose of them will be like dancing through the katas and not practicing the techniques. To fully practice your katas visualize an attacker for each move. Use power and concentrate on each technique, rather than see how fast you can get through the kata. Break down each move of the kata and look at the bunkai for each technique. In doing so, you will find many different applications for each move.

Looking at katas in this way will open your eyes to many other tuite techniques. ***Question: When is a block not really a block? Answer: When it could be tuite.*** When you look beyond the obvious you will find many hidden techniques within your katas and tuite is just one aspect.

Once you start looking at your katas' techniques and "look outside the kata box", you will find different bunkai for many of the techniques. Tuite plays a huge role in how many of these techniques work. If you find yourself wondering why a kata ends with a block… try looking at the end technique in a different light. You just might find that a block is not really a block after all.

Chapter 4 – Warm-ups and Stretches

Warm-ups and stretching are important elements of tuite practice and extremely important for both partners to prevent injury. There is a big difference between warm-ups and stretches. Warm-ups should always be performed prior to doing stretches.

The main purpose of warm-ups is to increase blood circulation in order to raise the temperature of the joints, muscles, tendons and ligaments. Tuite warm-ups target the anatomy most used during practice and the likelihood of injury is reduced. Warm-ups also reduce the severity of muscle soreness the next day. The increased blood flow resulting from warm-ups are important for the delivery of more oxygen to the joints, muscles, tendons and ligaments.

Stretching also increases blood circulation and raises the temperature of the joints, muscles, tendons and ligaments, although not as much as warm-ups. Stretching can help in flexibility and range of motion by lengthening muscles and tendons. The increased blood circulation can result in more energy. Stretches should be held for at least 30 seconds for best results and be completed before and after Tuite workouts.

Partners should massage each other's wrists during workouts to keep the joints loose and flexible.

Tuite Warm-ups

1 – Wrists up and down.
Briskly use an up and down motion using only the wrists 10 count.

2 – Wrists side to side Palms facing each other with fingers forward. Use a side to side motion using the wrists 10 count.

3 – Finger curls with palms up. Slowly tighten both fists 10 count.

4 – Finger curls with palms down using fast motion tighten both fists 10 count.

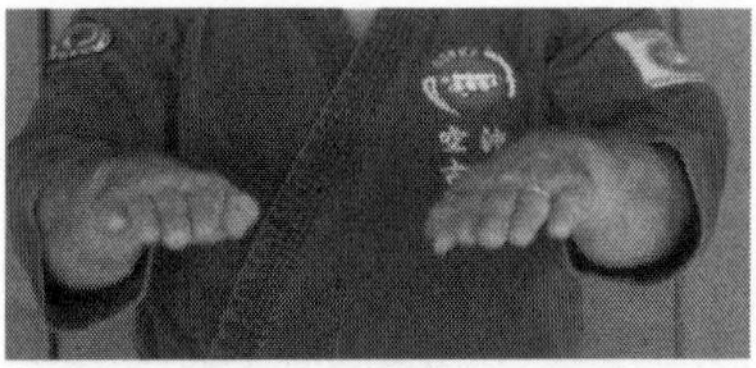

5 – Bicep curls palms up

Palms up and arms out, tighten fists and curl arms and wrists up 10 count.

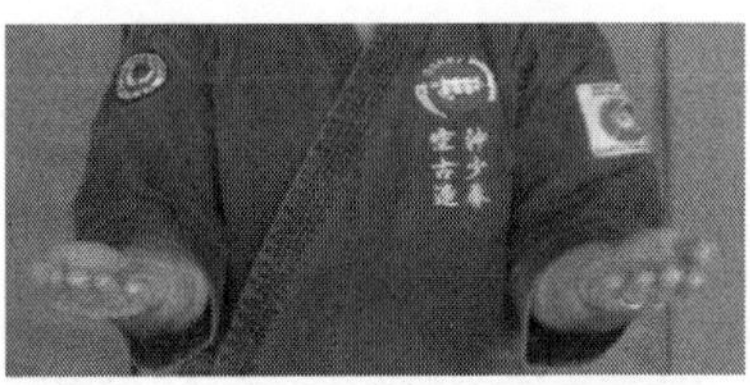

6 – Wrist rotations – Rotations forward and backward.

Using only the wrists, start with the palms in and rotating them inward 10 count and then outward 10 count.

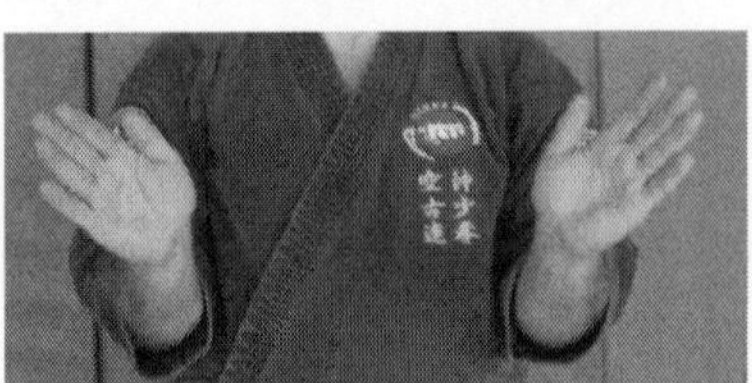

7 – Elbow rotations – Rotations forward and backward.

Using only the elbows, start with palms in and rotating them inward 10 count and then outward 10 count.

8 –Arm rotations – Forward and backward.

Using the whole arm with the hands in front of your obi (belt) rotate the arms at the shoulder in a big circle 10 count forward then 10 count backward.

9 – Neck exercises – Neck rotations – Clockwise 10 count and counter clockwise 10 count with upright posture

Caution: Although this is one of the federation exercises, there is controversy as to the pros and cons of neck rotations. Please be very careful with this.

10 – Neck exercises – Side to front to Side.

11 – Neck exercises – Up and down.

12 – Neck exercises – Ear to shoulder to middle to shoulder.

13 – Trunk twists

Twisting at the hips and using a loose movement swinging the arms as you twist.

14 – Knee/ankle rotations – Clockwise and counter clockwise
Hand on knees, both knees together go clockwise then counter clockwise.

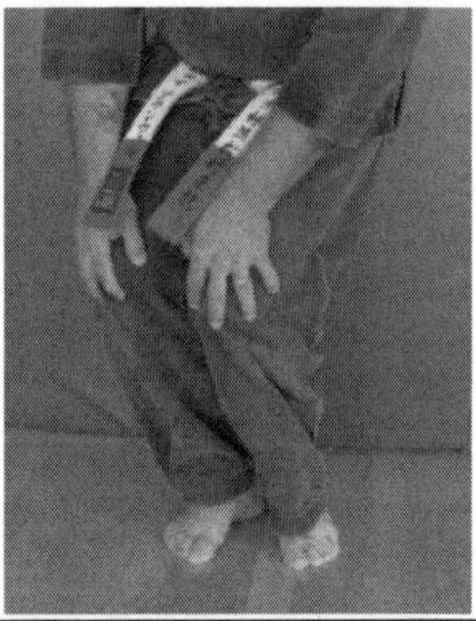	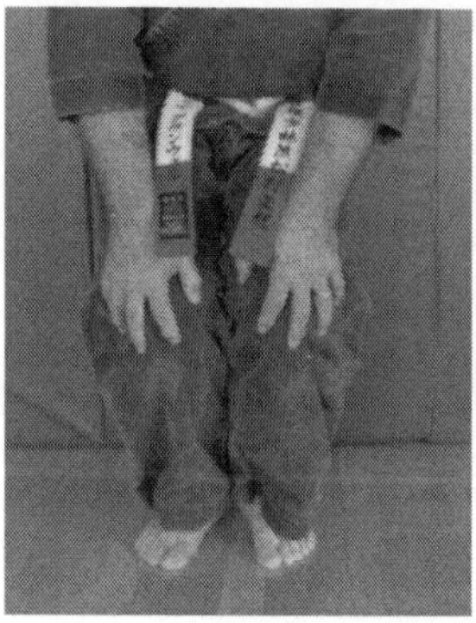
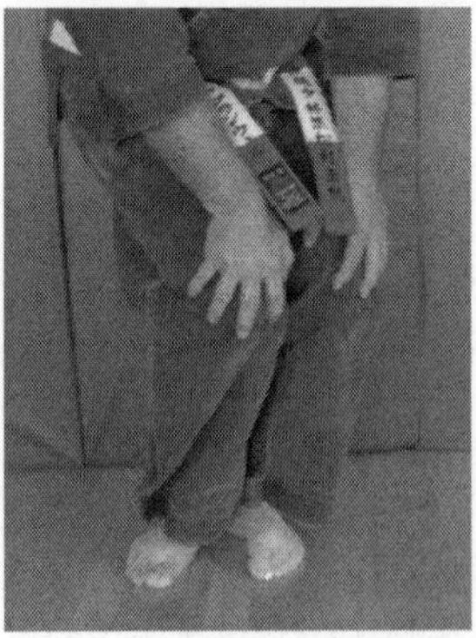	

15 –Knee/ankle rotations – In and out

Hands on knees, both knees together go in, then out then out then in.

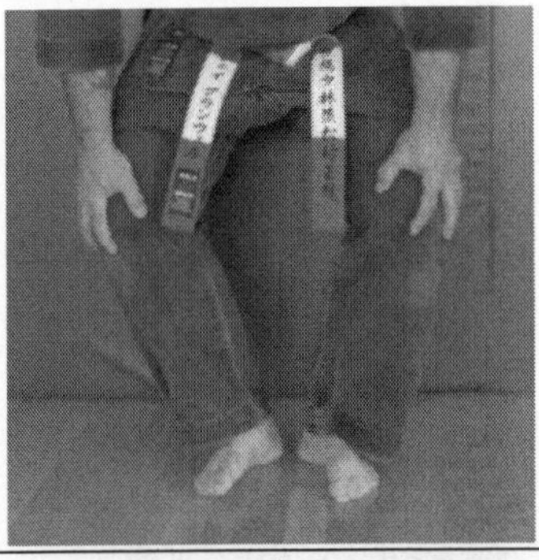

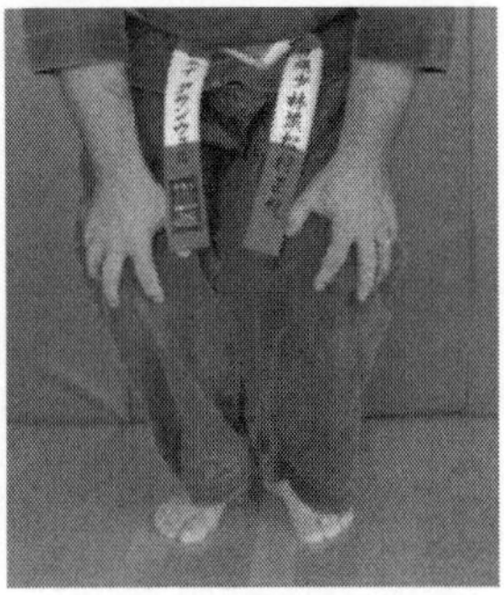

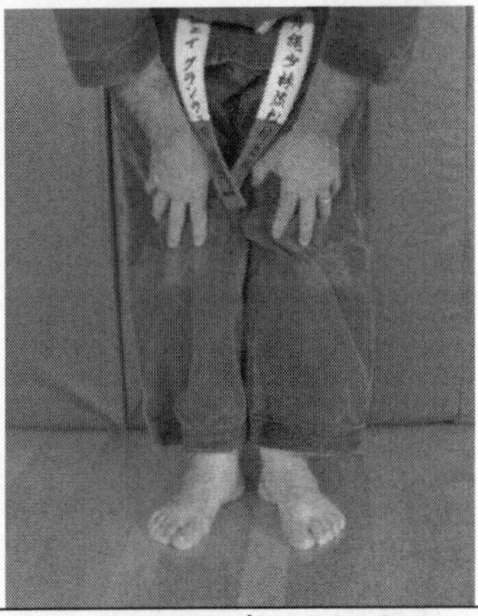

16 – Outside/inside foot turns

Hands on hips use ankles and turn the ankles outside then inside turning the feet in and out.

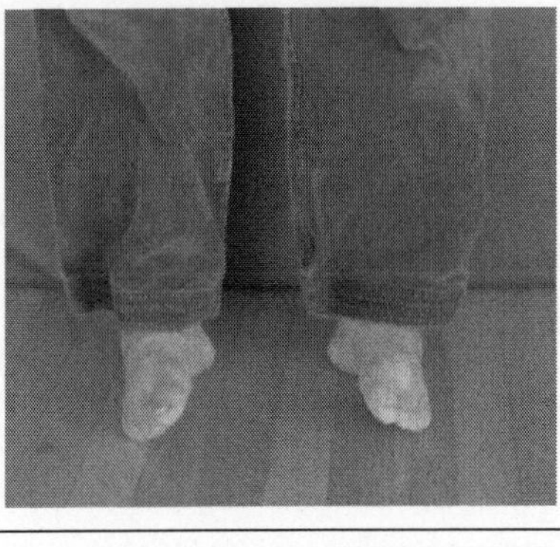

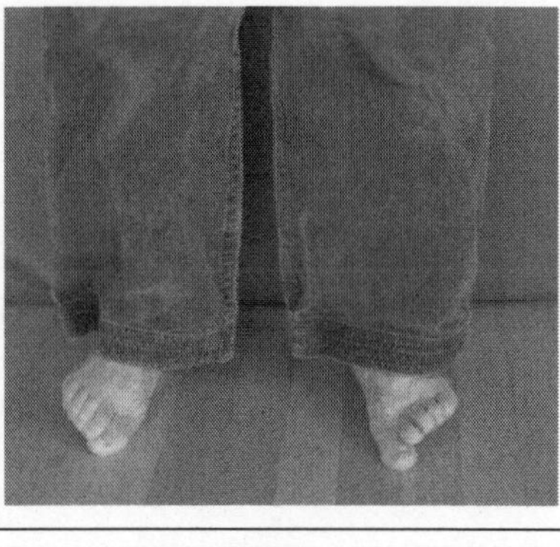

Tuite Stretches

Note: *While doing all stretches, apply pressure with opposite hand.*

1 – Left hand wrist out turn and outside ankle stretches.

At the same time do a wrist out turn and turn both feet on to the outer portion.

2 – Right hand wrist out turn and inside ankle stretch

At the same time do a wrist out turn and turn both feet inward.

3 – Left hand goose neck and toe stretch.

At the same time do a left handed goose neck and curl left toes up like a front snap kick.	

4 – Right hand goose neck and toe stretch.

At the same time do a right handed goose neck and curl right toes up like a front snap kick.	

5 – Extended wrist and toe stretch

At the same time with left hand extended, bend palm down and apply inward pressure and curl toes under.

Repeat using right hand and right toes.

6 – Extended – Palm up

Left hand extend arm forward, bend palm up

Palm face forward

7 – Extended – Palm down

Right hand extend arm forward, bend palm down

Palm face forward

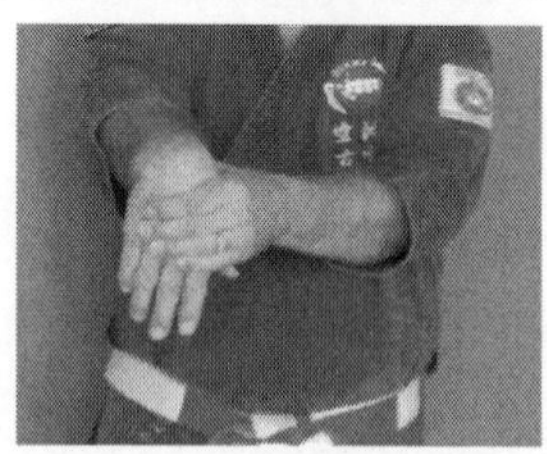

8 – Extended

Right hand extend arm forward, bend palm up Palm face forward	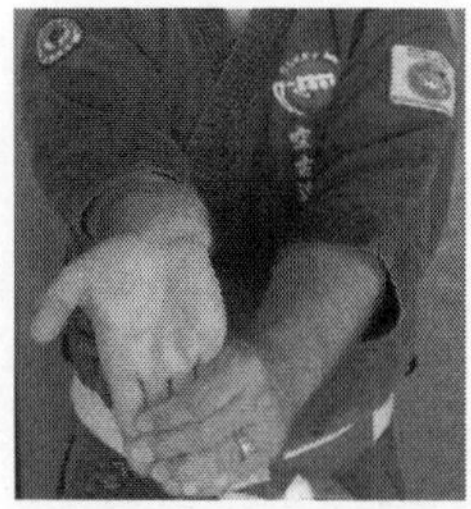

9 – Left hand thumb lock stretch

Right hand thumb lock stretch	

10 – Finger press

Contact with tips of finger only	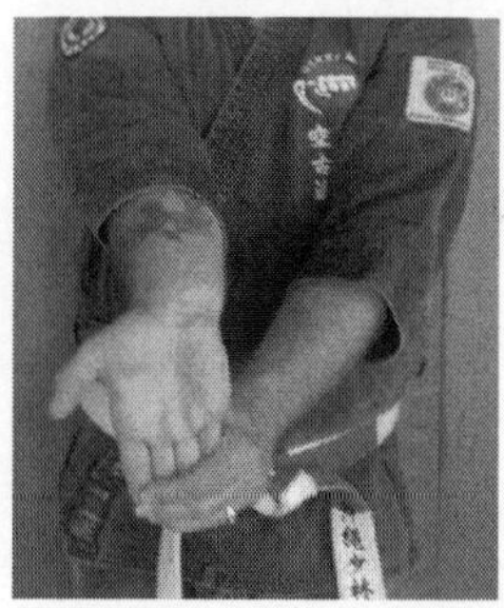

Chapter 5 – Tuite Techniques Explained

Several of the following techniques are used throughout the tuite sets. These are explained in detail here, so that they won't have to be explained in detail every time.

Goose Neck

Both the wrist and elbow are bent at 90 degree angles.	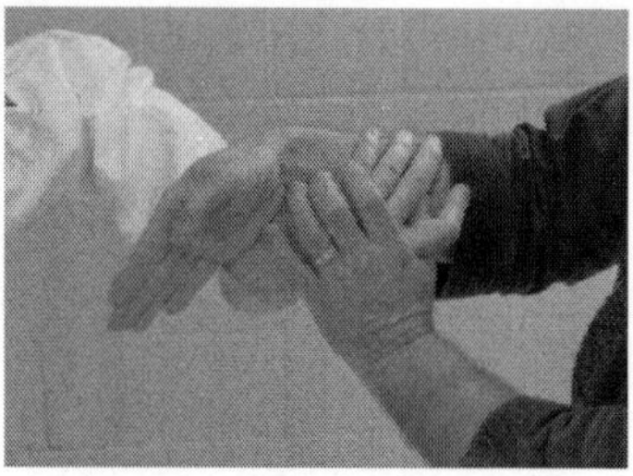

Wrist Out Grab #1

Firmly grab their palm side at the base of the thumb with your fingers.	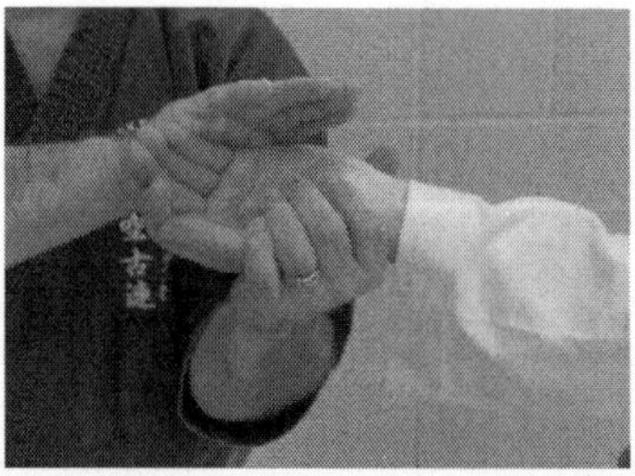
Grabbing their fingers twist the attacker's hand away from you and over with their palm down.	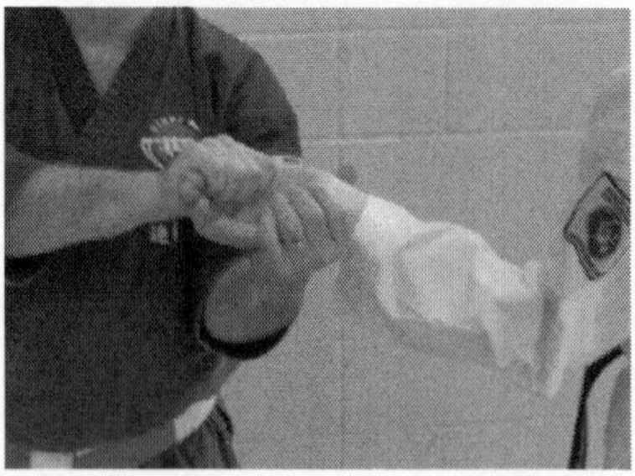

Wrist Out Grab #2

Firmly grab their palm side at the base of the thumb and base of their little finger with your fingers while pressing your thumbs on the back of their hand.	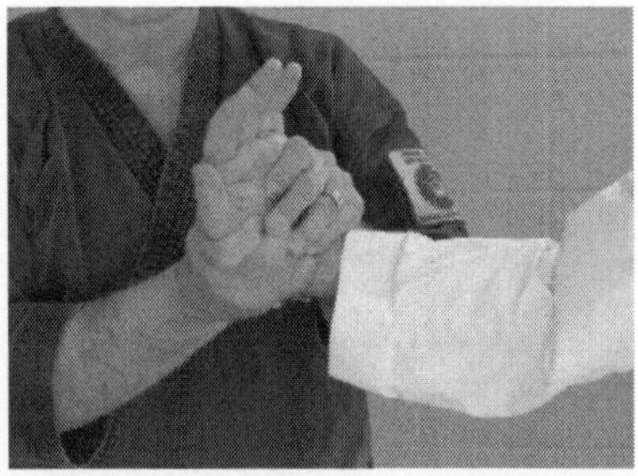
(Showing thumbs positions on the back of their hand.)	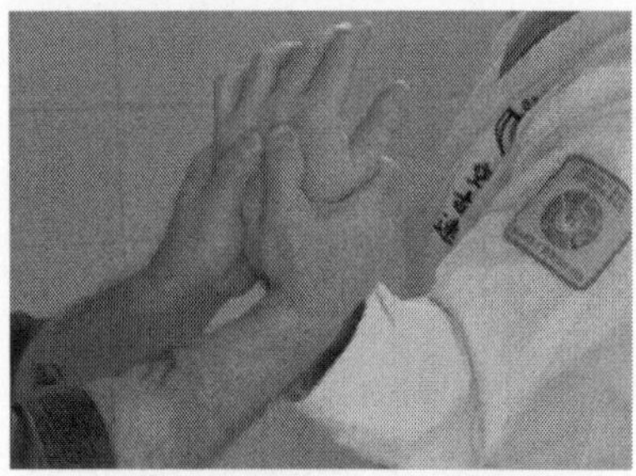
Twist the attacker's hand away from you and over with their palm down	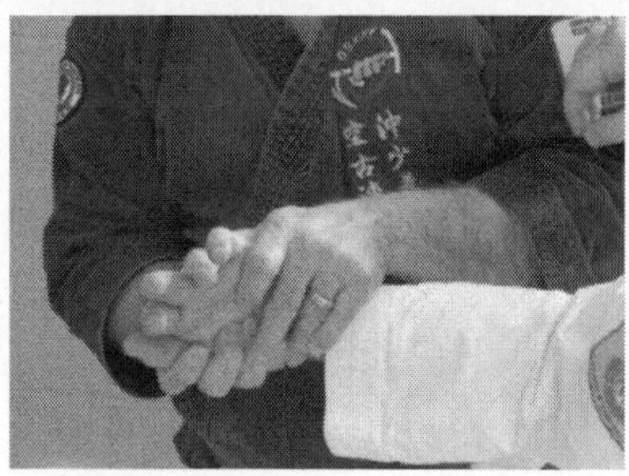

Wrist In Grab

With the attacker's palm facing up, grab firmly the base of the thumb on the palm side with your fingers. Press your thumbs on the back of their hand pressing down and toward their body.	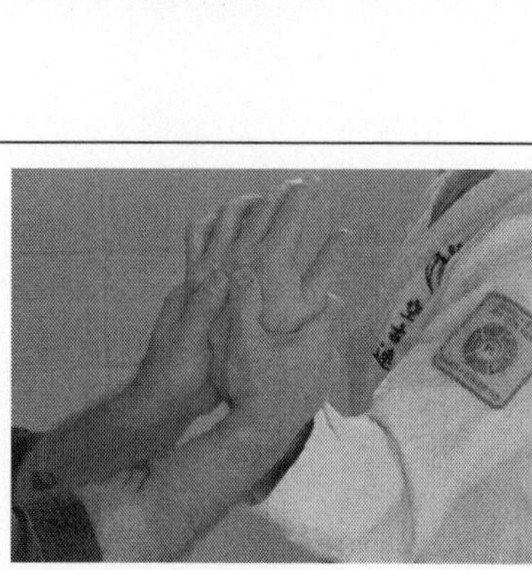

Arm Bar

Hold the attacker's wrist with one hand and put pressure on the back of their arm just above the elbow with your other hand.	

Arm Bar When Opponent On The Ground

With one foot under the attacker's shoulder blade, bend the attacker's wrist with their arm straight and pulling up with one hand, and put pressure on the back of their elbow with your knee.	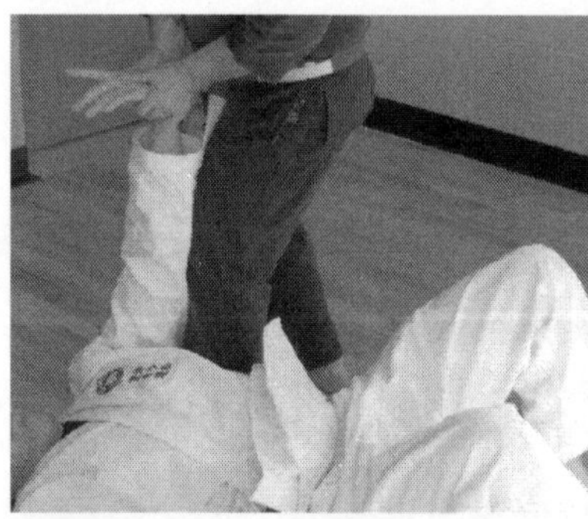
Note the position of your thumbs on the back of the attacker's hand.	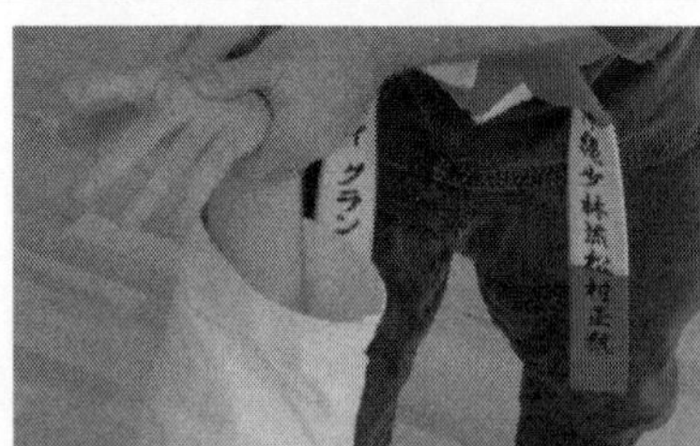

This is another type of arm bar with the attacker on the floor. This one uses your knee as a fulcrum on the attacker's elbow and the other knee on their shoulder pulling back on their hand.	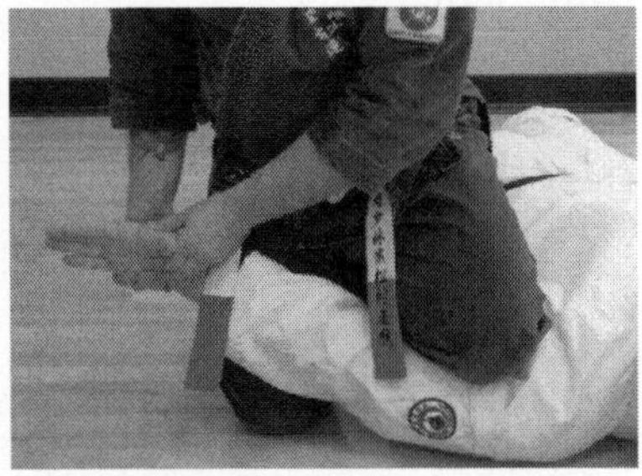

Bent Arm Bar When Opponent On The Ground

Using a Goose Neck on the ground, hold the attacker's wrist with one hand bending their wrist toward the back of their elbow, and put pressure on the back of their elbow with your knee.	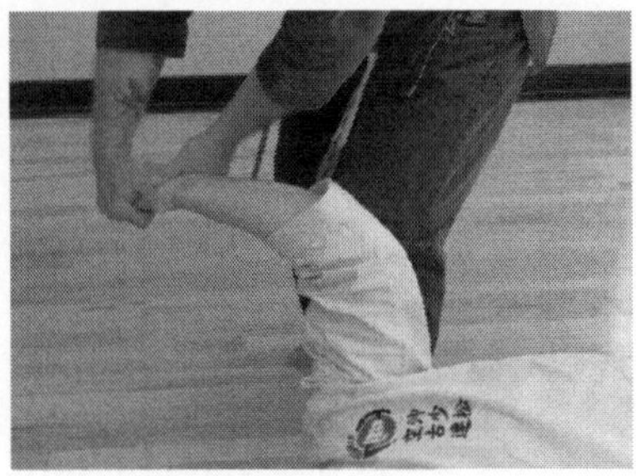

Hand Trap

One of the psychological aspects of karate is the hand trap. When someone grabs you and you put your hand on top of theirs, the mind plays a trick and causes them to hold on tighter and this is just what plays into your technique. In a lot of tuite, the tighter their grip, the better the technique works. With a hand trap you don't need to hold on so tight as to focus the opponent's attention to their grip. Instead their psychological process will cause them to hold tighter.

Notice this is not so much a physical hold, but a psychological hold.	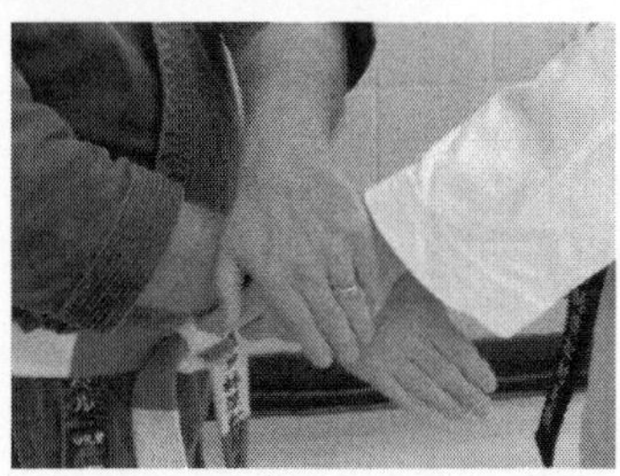

Hook Punch

The hook punch is not a tipical karate punch. It comes from the outside and is sometimes referred to as a haymaker or roundhouse. There are many techniques that use the arm grab and hook punch defenses.	

Change body

This is *not* a step back, but a slight change of the body to the side.

Starting position of change body.	
Position of change body. Notice the position of the feet. This is a short stance.	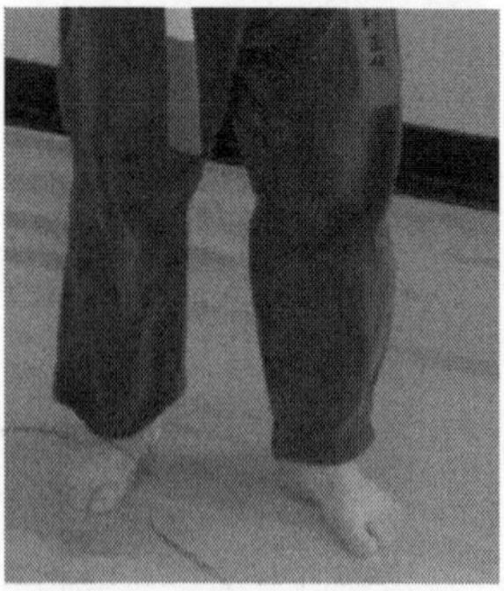

Note: *A long stance will cause you to be too far from the attacker and lose your advantage.*

Same Side Wrist Grab

This is a grab on the same side of body, i.e.; attacker's right hand grabbing your left hand.	

Cross Wrist Grab

This is a grab when the attacker grabs your wrist across your body i.e.; attacker's right hand grabbing your right hand.	

Chapter 6 - NorthWest Budokan Self Defense Set

NWB-1 – Same Side Wrist Grab

Single Same Side Wrist Grab	
Make a fist with the hand that was grabbed.	
Grab your own hand.	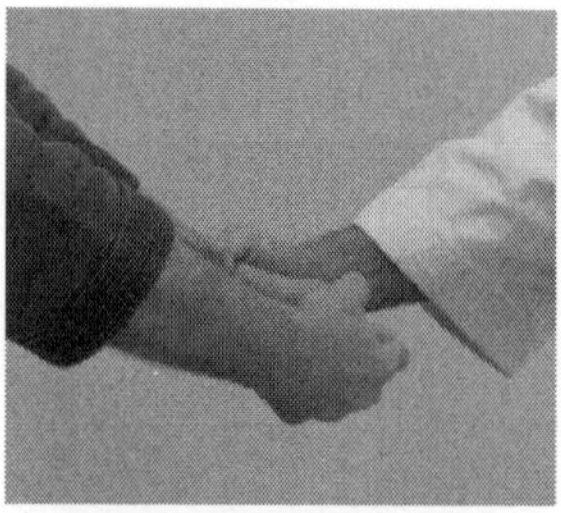
At the same time: Step back and pull your hand to the opposite shoulder of the arm that was grabbed.	

With the same hand that was grabbed, counter with a backfist to the attacker's face. *Note: If you step back to far shuffle forward in order to strike the attacker's face.*	

NWB-2 – Double Wrist Grab

Double Wrist Grab	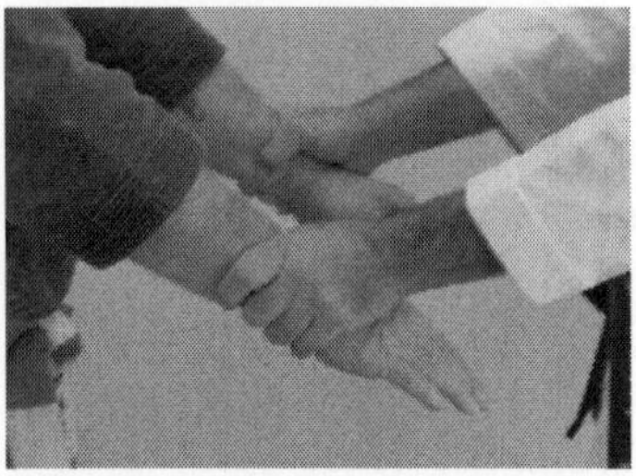
Turn your hands up, so your palms face up.	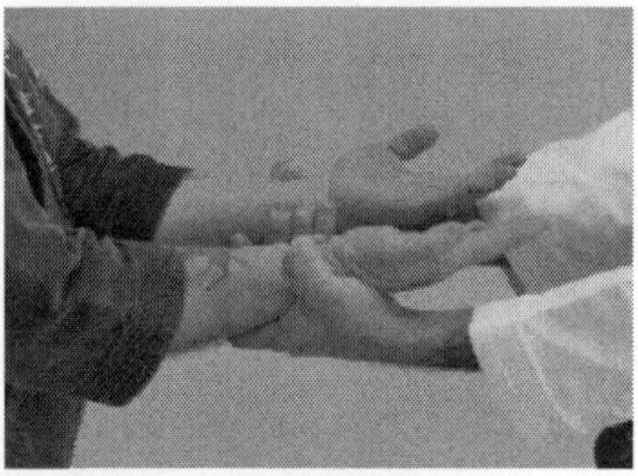
At the same time: Step back and bring your hands even with the sides of your head.	

Counter with a kick to attacker's groin. *Note: Be careful not to hit your face with hands. Go to the outside of your head.*	

NWB-3 – Front Choke

Front Choke *Note: For practice only put your hands on the shoulders. Do not really choke.*	
Put one arm up all the way.	
Step back with the opposite foot, and turn your body 90 degrees using your armpit to remove the attacker's hands. Making sure to always look at the attacker.	

With the arm that is up, strike the attacker's face with your elbow.	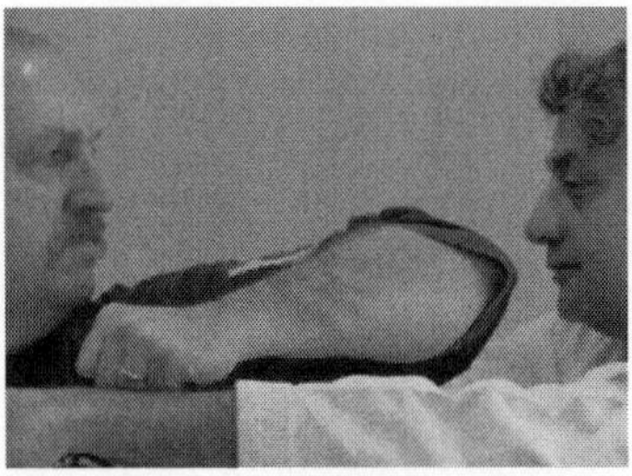

Note: If the attacker is tall then you can do an elbow strike to the attacker's ribs or dropping way down for a groin strike by going under the attacker's arms.

NWB-4 – Rear Choke

Rear Choke	
Put one arm up all the way and step forward with the opposite foot.	

Note: For both the front and back choke you must keep your arm ALL the way UP using your armpit to break the attacker's hold.

Make sure you look at the attacker and turn your body 90 degrees toward your back foot.	
Wrap your arm over the attacker's arm and trap their arms at the elbows.	
Counter with a punch to the attacker's ribs with your free hand.	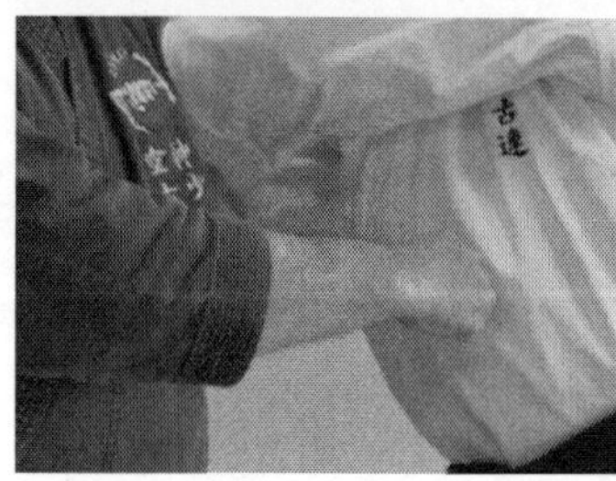

Note: For both the front and back choke you must keep your arm ALL the way UP using your armpit to break the attacker's hold.

Chapter 7 – OSMKKF Tuite

The following chapters are the tuite sets for the OSMKKF requirements for 10 kyu to 1 kyu as taught by Master Fusei Kise and Kaicho Isao Kise.

10 Kyu Tuite

10-1 - Same Side Single Wrist Grab

Same side single wrist grab	
Open your grabbed hand going underneath and to the outside of the attacker.	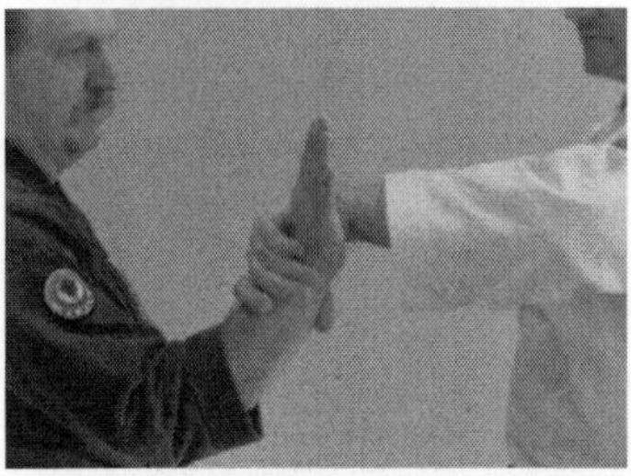
Keeping fingers together, continue to circle the hand over the top of the attacker's hand with your thumb up, pressing the bottom edge on your hand against attacker's wrist.	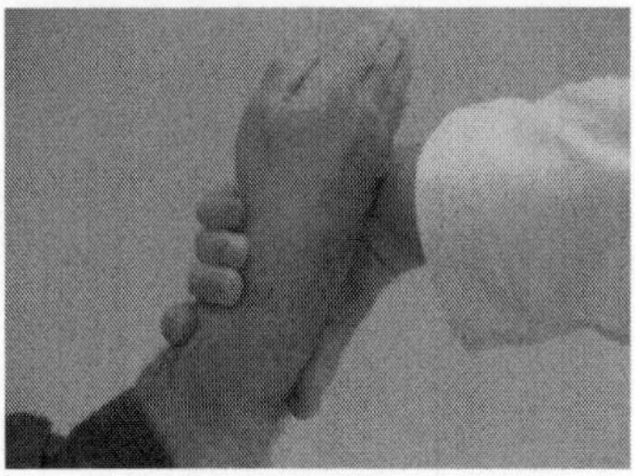

Continue with spear hand to attacker's solar plexus.	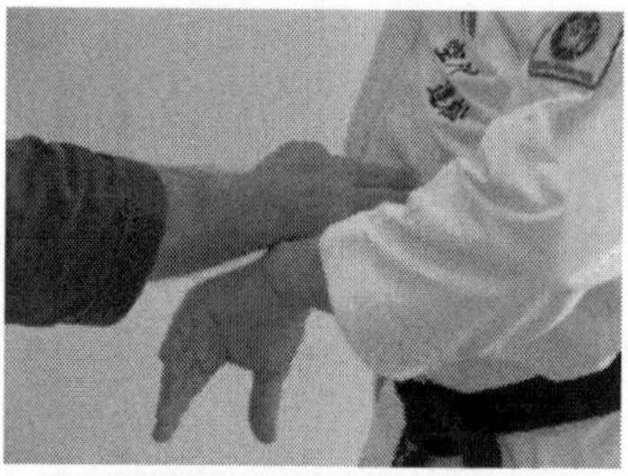

10-2 - Cross Wrist Grab

Cross wrist grab	
Open your grabbed hand going underneath and to the outside of the attacker.	
Keeping fingers together, continue to circle the hand over the top of the attacker's hand with your thumb up and press the bottom edge on your hand against attacker's wrist.	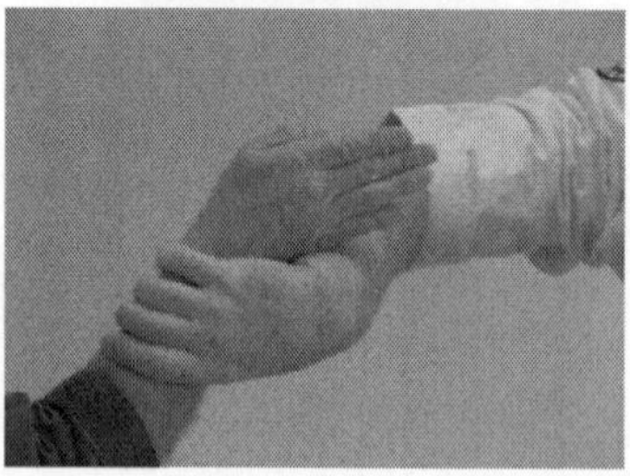

Continue with spear hand to attacker's solar plexus.	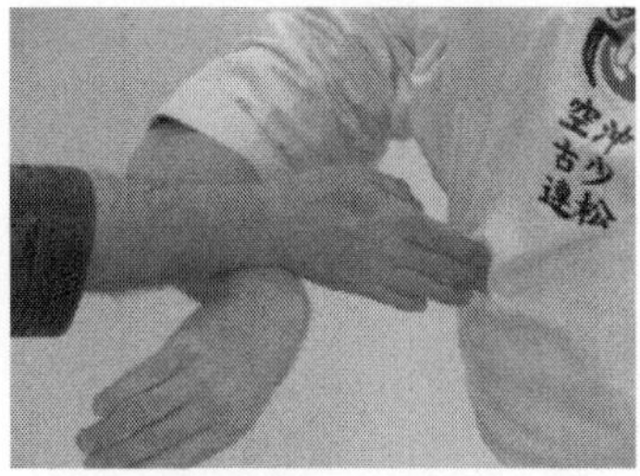

10-3 - Double Wrist Grab

Double wrist grab	
Open your grabbed hands going underneath and to the outside of both the attacker's hands.	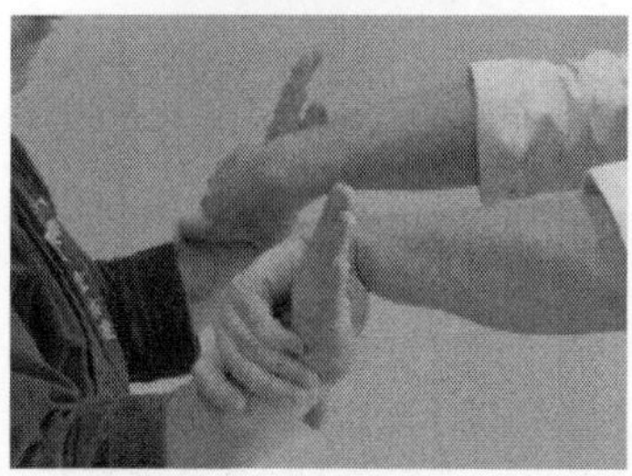
Continue to circle the hand over the top of the attacker's hand with your thumbs up, pressing the bottom edge of your hands against attacker's wrists.	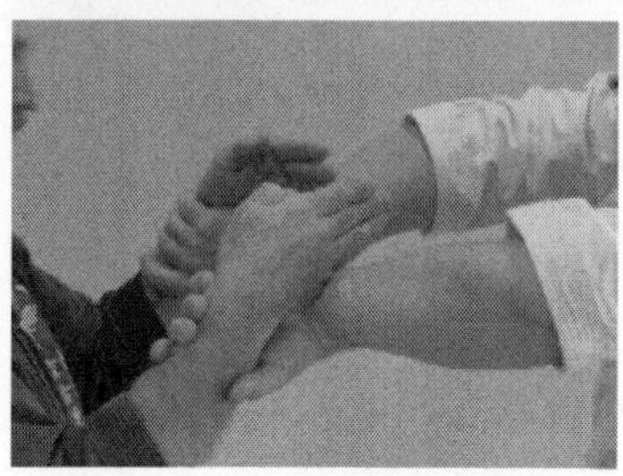

Continue with spear hands to attacker's solar plexus.	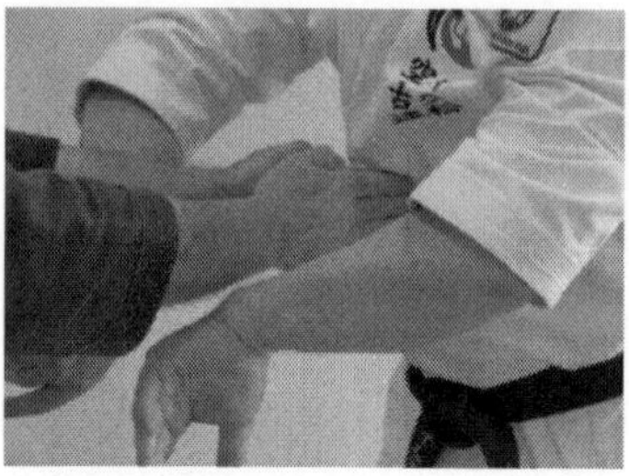

10-4 – First 3 Fast

Number 1, 2 & 3: Single hand grab, reverse hand grab and double hand grab. (See pictures for #10-1 thru 10-3)

10-5 - Same Side Wrist Grab

Same side wrist grab	
Make a fist then open your fist. This makes your wrist smaller.	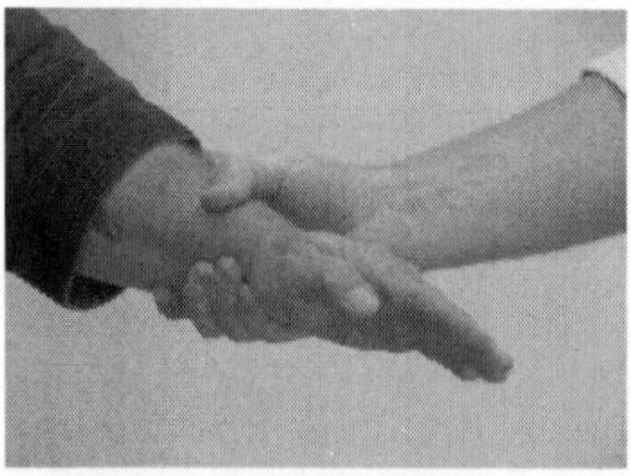
Turn your wrist slightly, so the thinnest part of your wrist is between the attacker's thumb and forefinger.	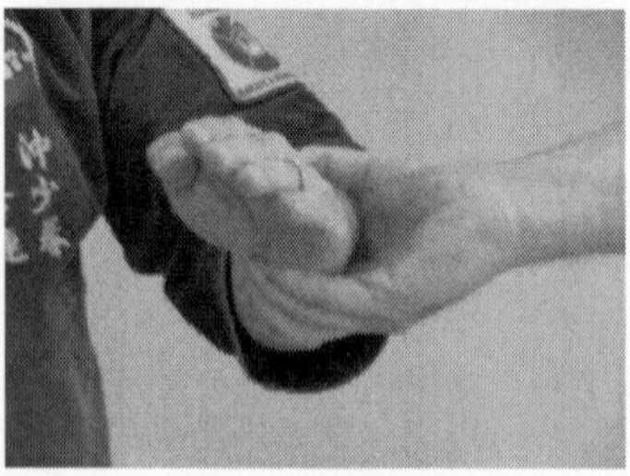

At the same time: pull your hand up to your opposite shoulder and change body. Follow with a back fist. *Note: This is a **change body** and not a step back.*	

Chapter 8 - 9th Kyu Tuite

9-1 - Same Side Wrist Grab

Same side wrist grab	
Bring your palm up, so you're looking at your own palm solar plexus high with your other hand, thumb up, under the attacker's wrist joint.	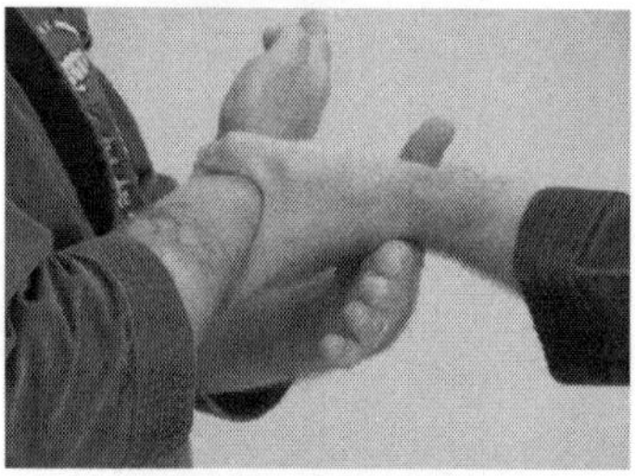
At the same time: step back and roll your grabbed hand down to the attacker's fingers.	
Pushing against the attacker's fingers and pulling against their wrist, step forward applying upward pressure. *Note: Do not raise your hands above your solar plexus.*	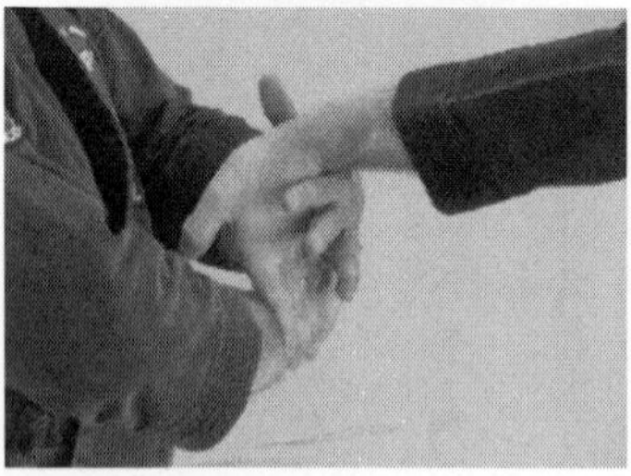

9-2 - Same Side Elbow Grab

Same side elbow grab	
Grab the attacker's wrist (thumb up or down) with your middle finger in their wrist joint.	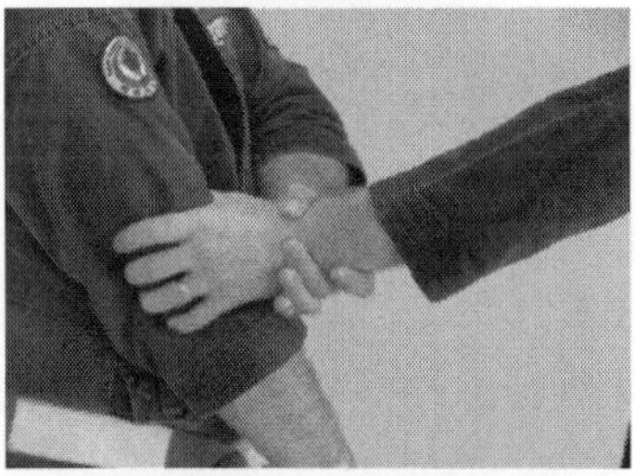
Bend your elbow out just a bit and step back to straighten the attacker's arm.	
Pull the attacker's wrist toward your body and shuffle forward pushing against their fingers with your elbow. *Note: Pulling the attacker's wrist to the side will only cause them to walk around you. It's very important to pull the attacker's wrist toward you and not around you.*	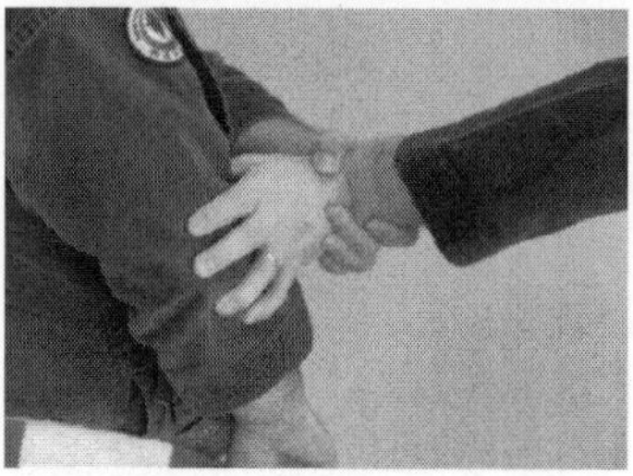

9-3 - One Hand Lapel Grab

One hand lapel grab	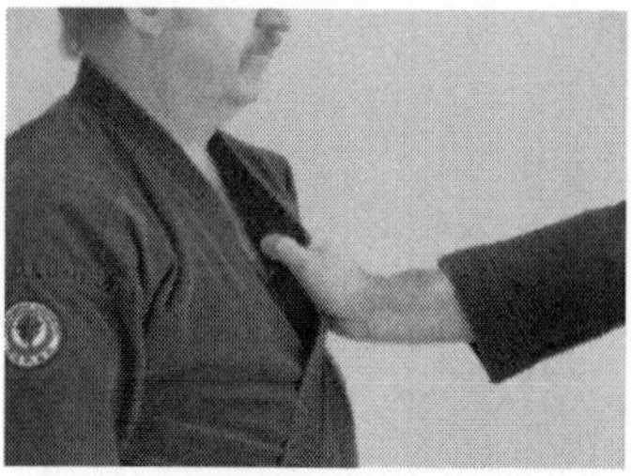
At the same time: grab the attacker with the same side hand under the elbow and with the other hand administer a thumb compression.	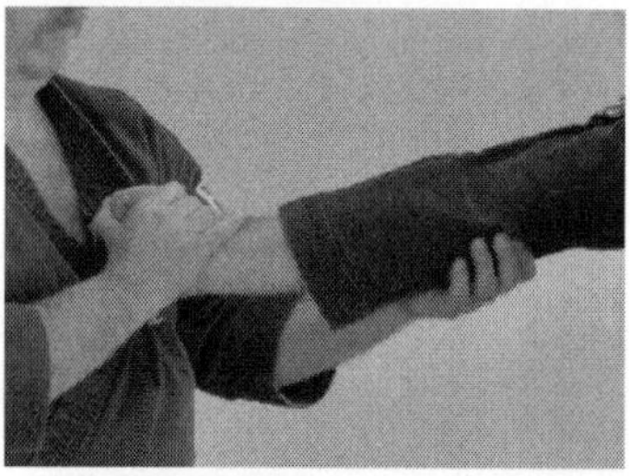
Thumb compression: press your thumb against the tip of the attacker's thumb and compress their thumb with your other fingers. *Note: If their hand is a lot bigger you can also use your palm instead of your thumb.*	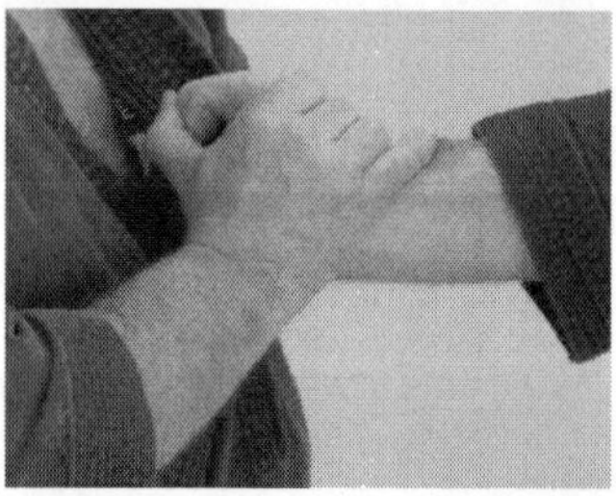
Elbow pressure point: this is located just above the elbow. Apply pressure with your fingers in a claw like grip.	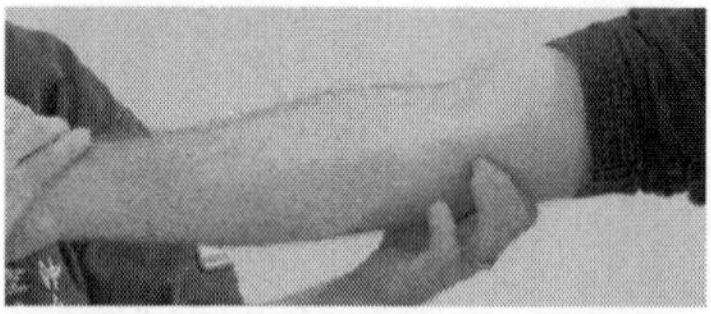
Change body to straighten the attacker's arm. *Note: Pressure points can be hard to hit and if it doesn't seem to work grab the muscle hard and twist.*	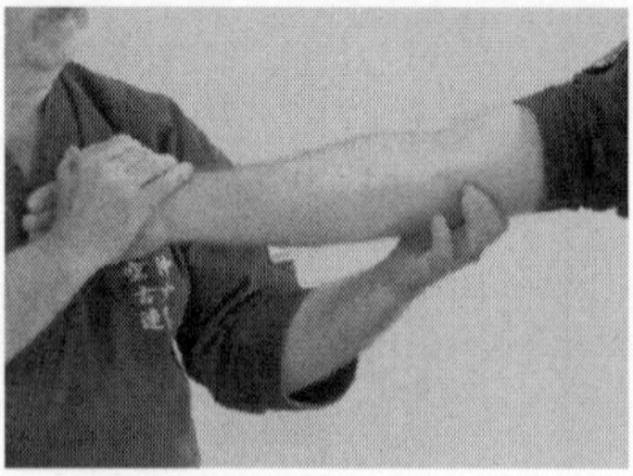

9-4 - Same Side Shoulder Grab

Same side shoulder grab	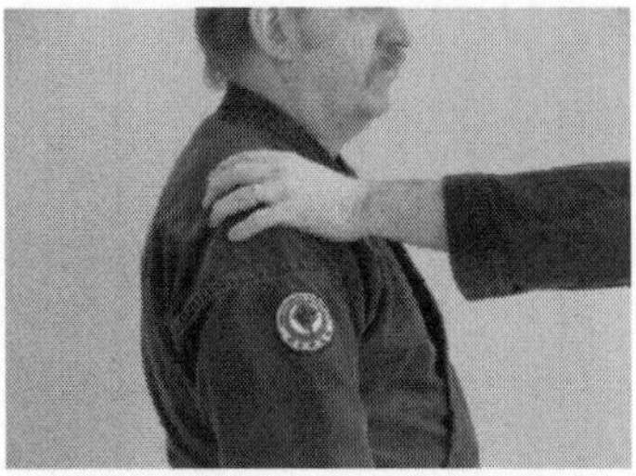
Place your opposite hand on your attacker's hand. *Note: Placing your hand on an attacker will cause them to hold tighter. This is a psychological aspect and is used several times in tuite.*	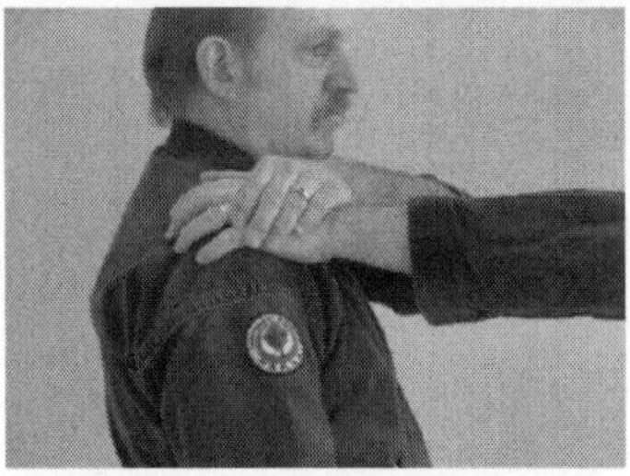
Press their hand against your shoulder, keeping their thumb down.	
Raise your arm and using your arm, push down on top of the attacker's arm.	

Chapter 9 - 8th Kyu
Self Defense Set #1 (1 thru 5)

The Self Defense Set is a set of ten techniques with the first five being the requirements for 8th Kyu and the last five for 7th Kyu. The techniques are using tuite techniques and introduce some of the range of motion for joints and change body.

8-1 - Same Side Wrist Grab

Same side wrist grab	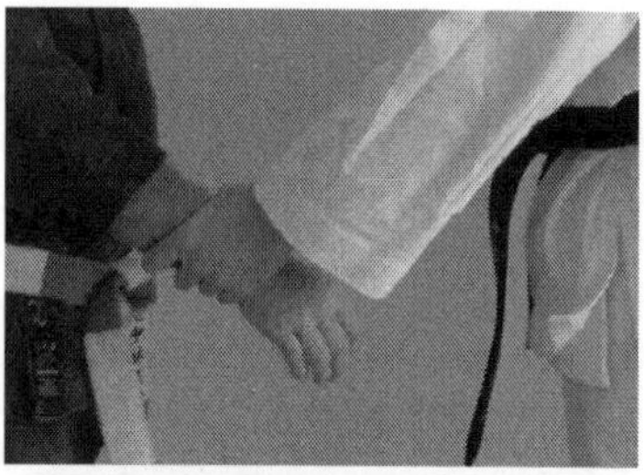
At the same time: Front kick to the attacker's opposite thigh of the side that was grabbed and step back to a change body and...	
On the attacker's hand, grab their hand and press your thumb on the point between the thumb and forefinger.	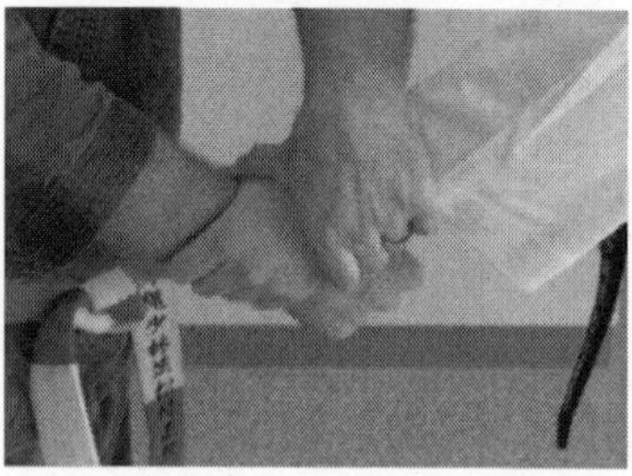

Make a big circle to the outside bringing your hands in as you would catch a football and with your thumb initiate a thumb lock on the attacker.	
Make sure your other wrist is all the way down in the the area between the attacker's thumb and fore finger.	
The attacker should now be bent over in a arm bar with their palm up. Using pressure of your wrist use your elbow to bend and point their thumb at their nose. *Note: Make sure you do not bend over.*	
Finish with a second kick.	

8-2 - Same Side Elbow Grab

Same side elbow grab	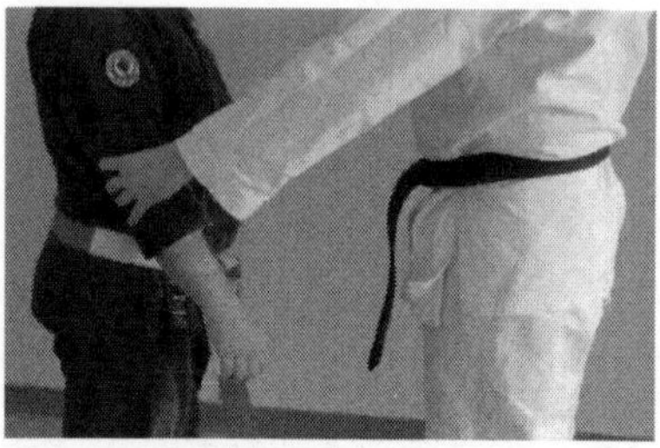
At the same time: On the attacker's hand, grab their hand and press your thumb on the point between the thumb and forefinger initiating a thumb lock on the attacker and...	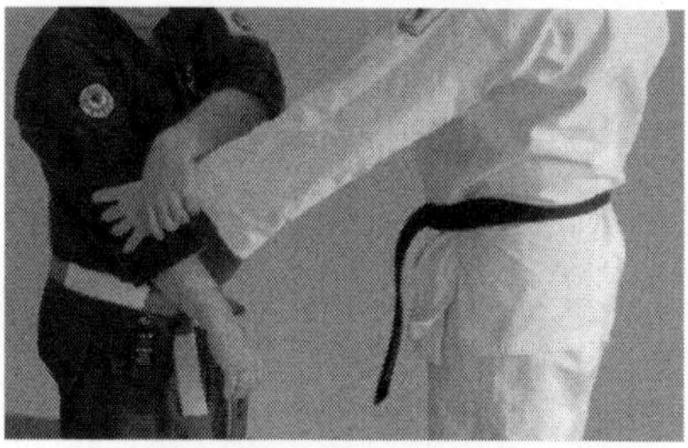
Front kick to the attacker's opposite thigh of the side that was grabbed and after kicking step back to a change body and with your hand, of the side that was grabbed, straighten their elbow with a hard palm strike upwards.	
Using the same hand and using the base in a knife hand at the point just above their elbow, roll their arm into an arm bar.	

Note: Make sure the attacker's elbow is lower than their hand keeping their hand close to your own body.	
Finish with a second kick.	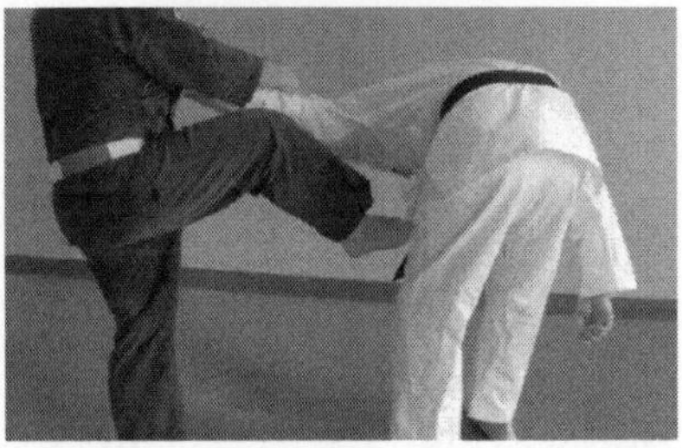

8-3 - Same Side Shoulder Grab

Same side shoulder grab	
At the same time: Front kick to the attacker's opposite thigh of the side that was grabbed and after kicking step back to a change body and on the attacker's hand, grab their hand and press your thumb on the point between the thumb and forefinger.	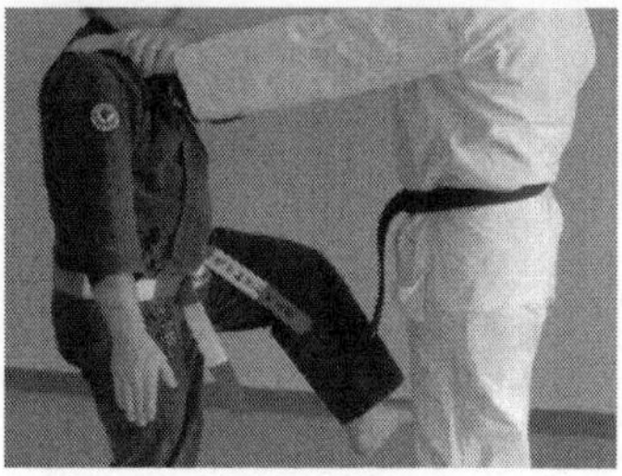

Using the hand on the side that was gabbed, strike their arm close to the shoulder with a palm strike coming from the outside just below their shoulder to dislocate their shoulder.	
Using the same hand, initiate an arm bar and with the other hand initiate a thumb lock and wrist lock.	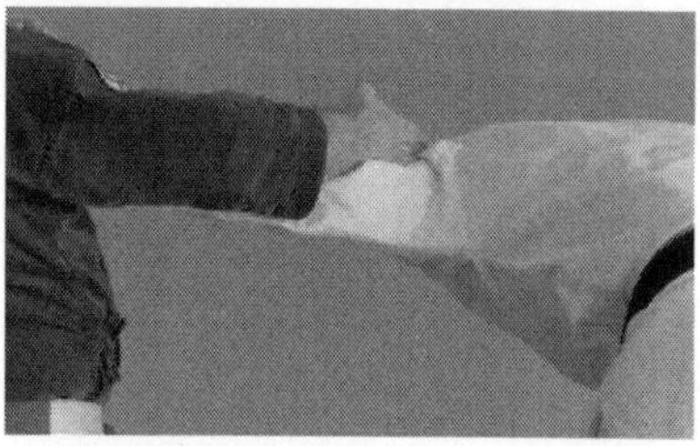
Shuffle in pressing your hand into their shoulder joint and causing them to bend down. *Note: Make sure the attacker's elbow is lower than their hand keeping their hand close to your own body.*	
Finish with a second kick.	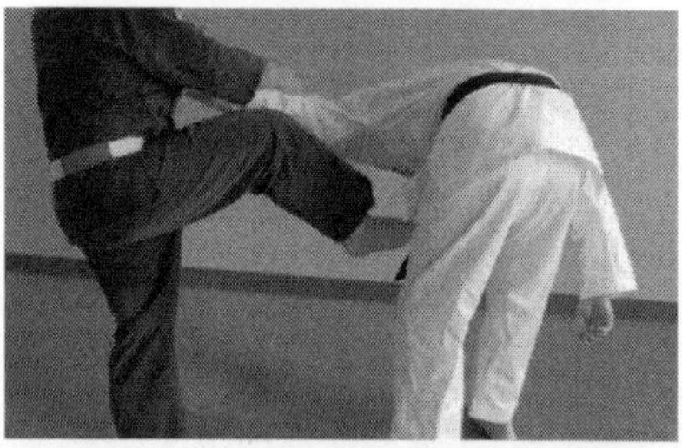
If they try to raise up press your finger into the pressure points in the side of their neck.	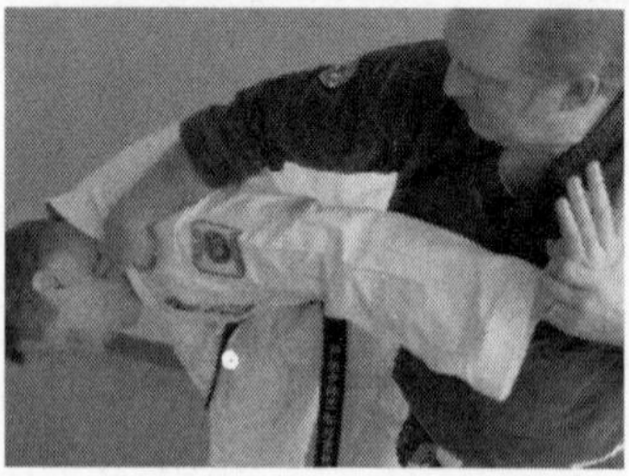

8-4 - Two Hand Choke

<table>
<tr><td>Attacker steps forward and reaches for a two hand choke.</td><td>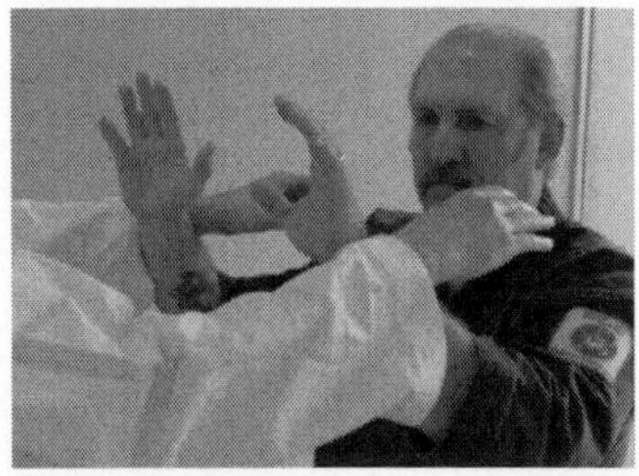</td></tr>
<tr><td>At the same time: Bring both your hands up between the attacker's reached out hands blocking with the back of your hands facing you and kick to the attacker's back leg stepping forward(White Crane stance).

Note: It's very important that you keep your hands and arms up and don't drop them.</td><td></td></tr>
<tr><td>With either hand, grab their wrist sliding down to a wrist lock.</td><td>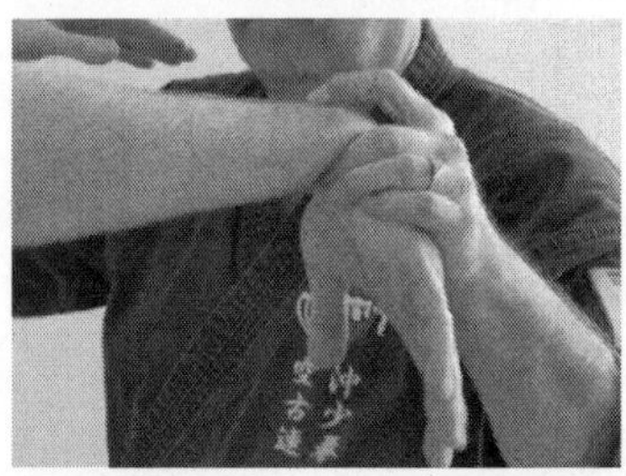</td></tr>
<tr><td>With the other hand strike with a back fist or punch to the temple or to the face whichever is your preference.</td><td></td></tr>
</table>

8-5 - Bear Hug From Behind

Bear hug from behind	
Using the side of your foot, scrape down the attacker's shin and end by stomping on their instep and stepping out.	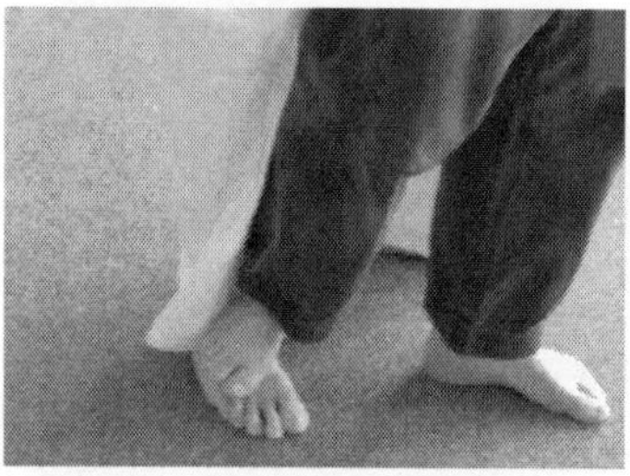
At the same time: Bring your arm up, as you would a high block breaking the attacker's hold and use the other arm for an elbow strike into the attacker's solar plexus.	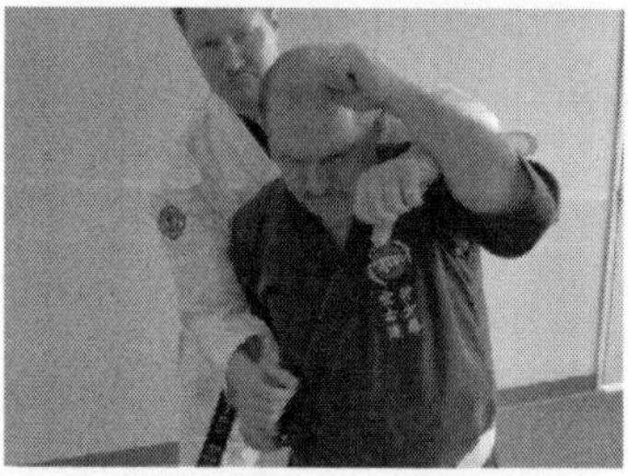
Note: It's very important that you tuck your chin to your chest to prevent the attacker choking you when their arms come up.	

With the hand that was used for the elbow strike, strike to the attacker's groin and...	
...then do an uppercut. *Note: Remember to strike always the groin first. This causes the attacker's head to come forward and gives you a great target. Striking the head first only causes the attacker to fall backward.*	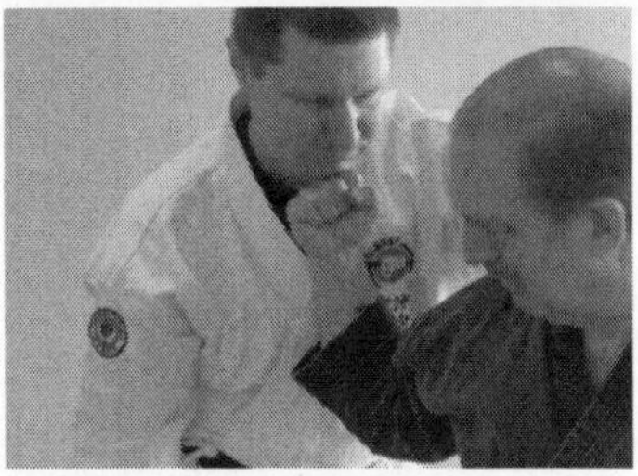
Finish with a back kick to the attacker.	

Chapter 10 - 7th Kyu Self Defense # 2 (6 thru 10)

7-6 - Buddy Grab

Buddy grab	
At the same time: With the hand next to the attacker, reach behind and using your middle finger, poke them hard in the side below the ribs and...	
...reach up with your other hand grabbing with a wrist out grab, turn the attacker's hand counterclock wise until their palm is up.	
Bend your legs just a bit and center the attacker's elbow on the back of your neck. While standing back up pull down on the attacker's arm. *Note: Be very careful when practicing this with a partner. Pulling down on the arm bar can cause the elbow to be hyperextended.*	

7-7 - Hair Grab

Hair Grab with one hand.	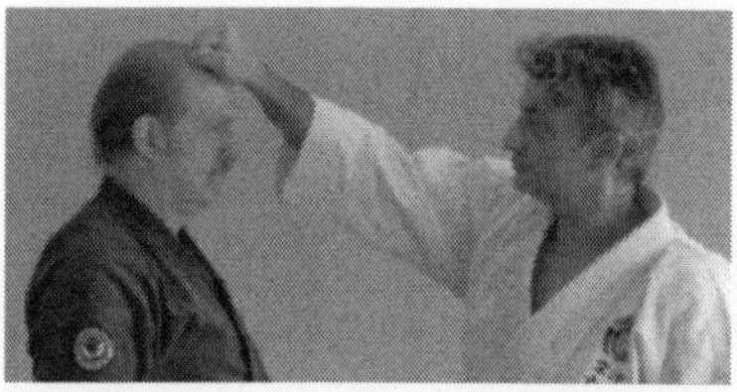
Place both hands, palms crossing and facing you, on the attacker's wrist.	
Press the attacker's hand hard against your head.	
At the same time: Take a big step back and bend over about to the attacker's knee level.	

7-8 - Shaking Hands

Shaking hands	
Lift the attacker's hand up and with your opposite foot step forward and close to their body keeping their palm up.	
Pivot so you're facing the same way as the attacker placing their arm on your shoulder and pulling down.	

With your other hand strike to the groin then strike to the face of the attacker.

7- 9 - Double Lapel Grab

Double lapel grab	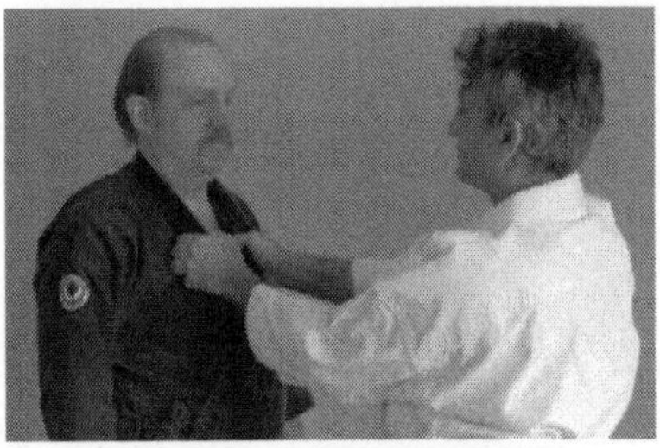
With both hands, place your hands on the top of the attacker's and using wrist out grabs with your thumbs on the middle of the back of their hands.	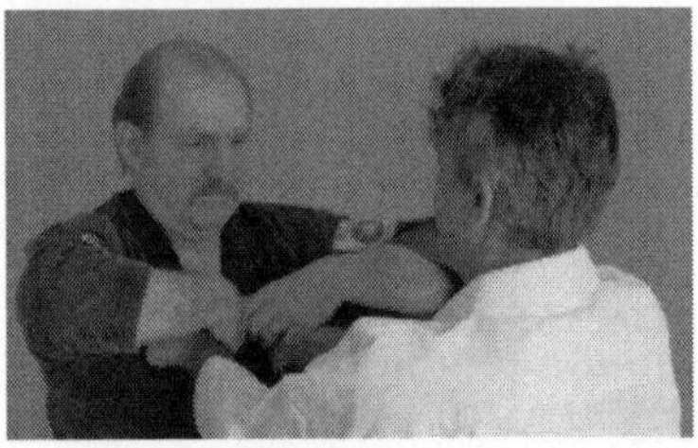
Turn both of the attacker's hands over, palms facing toward the attacker and twist down.	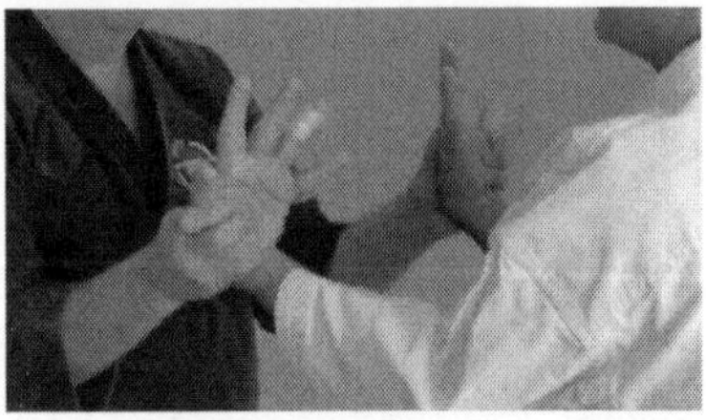
Without completely letting go, grab the attacker's thumbs and apply pressure down and pulling to the outside.	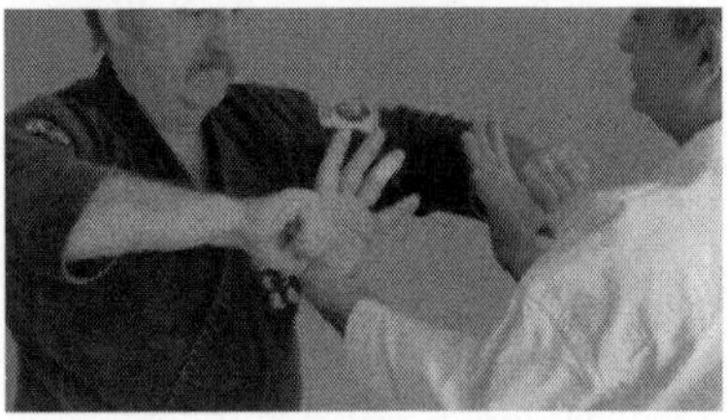

7-10 - Stepping Forward Punch

Stepping forward punch	
Change body blocking the punch with a knife hand at the forarm and grab the attacker's arm.	
At the same time: Continue stepping around, so you are facing the same way as the attacker and place your other hand just above the elbow using the base of your hand. Initiate an arm bar keeping the attacker's wrist close to your body and forcing the attacker down.	

Chapter 11 - 6th Kyu Tuite

6-1 – Front Choke

Reaching forward as if going to choke.	
Grab the attacker's hands so you are palm to palm and their thumbs are between your thumbs and fore fingers.	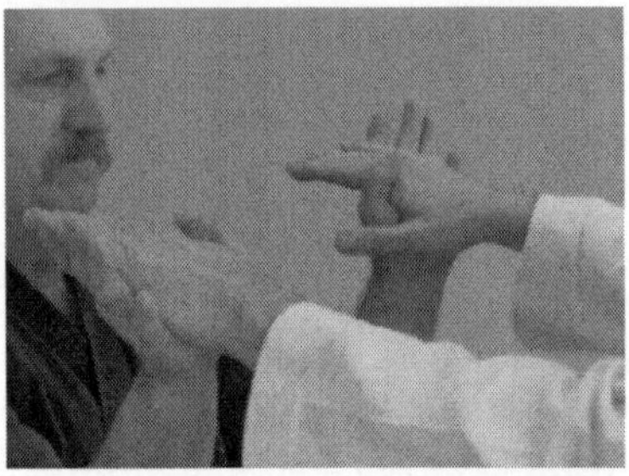
Making a big arc to the outside turn both the attacker's hands over, keeping their elbows bent.	
Apply pressure with your fingers forcing his little fingers down and across his ring fingers.	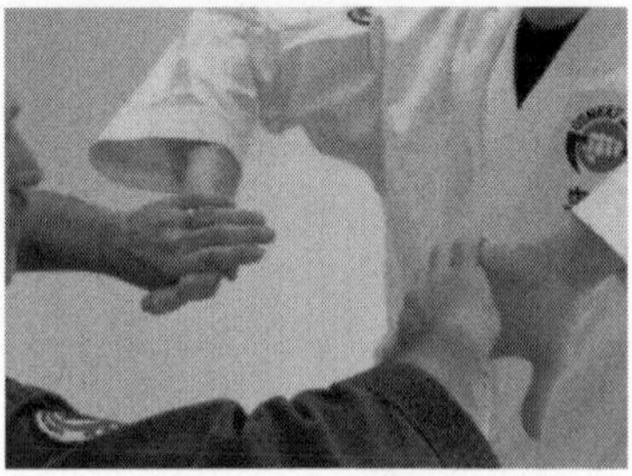

This causes the attacker to go down.	
A second way, especially if their arms are straight: Instead of turning the attacker's hands over is to put their hands back to back and to toark in a clockwise motion toward their body.	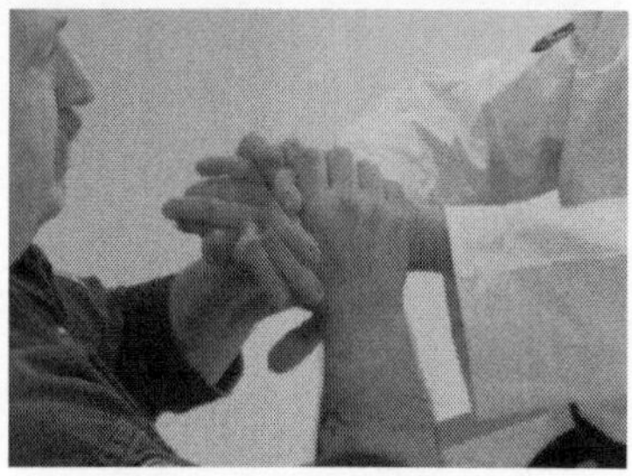

6-2 – Front Choke

Reaching forward as if going to choke.	
Grab the attacker's hands so you are palm to palm and with thumb between your thumbs and fore fingers.	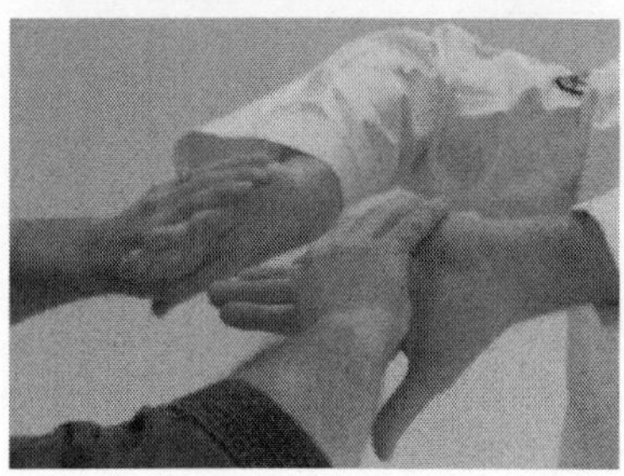

Stepping forward, make a big arc to the outside turning both the attacker's hands over, one at a time starting with the back hand and keeping his elbows bent.	
Apply pressure with your fingers forcing their little fingers down and across his ring fingers. Continue the circle and this will raise the attacker up.	

6-3 - Praying Hand Grab

Praying hand grab	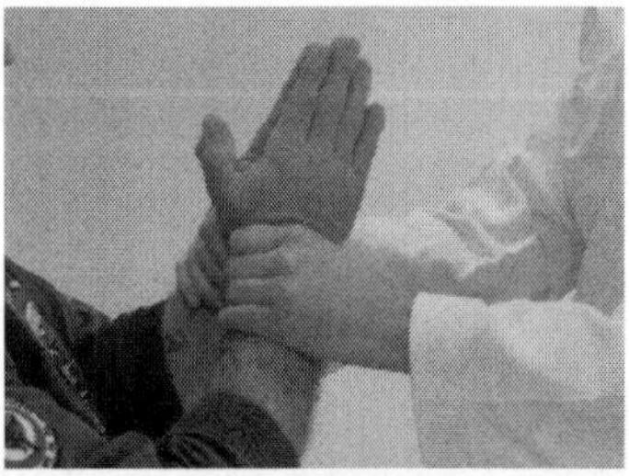
Step forward and spred the attacker's hands to the outside.	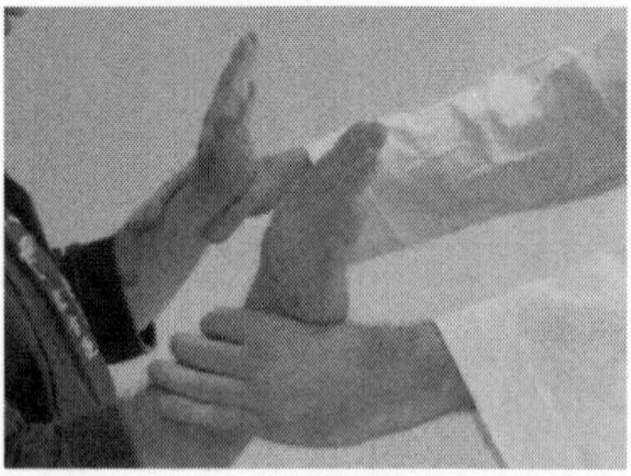

Bring your hands over and on top and into wrist locks on both their hands. Step back and slightly down, then stepping forward and using the palm of your hands against the back of the attacker's hand; force the attacker's arms up at a 45 degree angle.	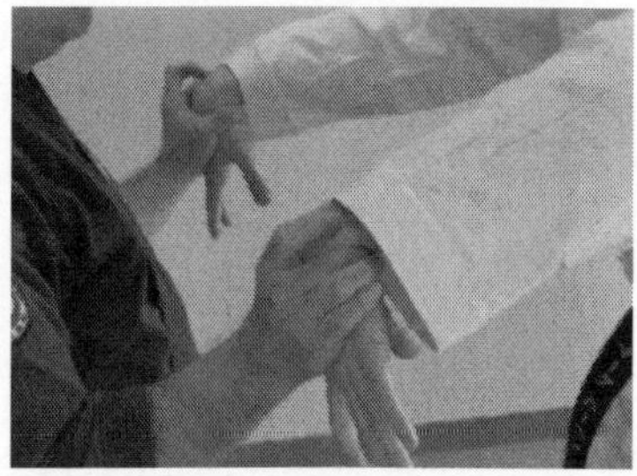
Option: To keep the attacker from going backward step on the attacker's foot between the 2nd and 3rd toes using your big toe.	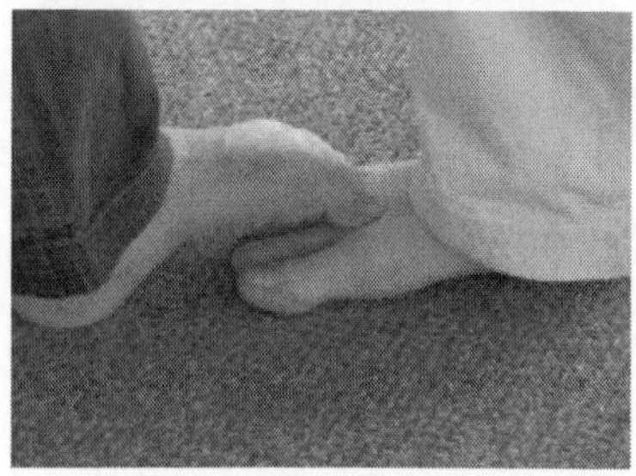

6-4 - Praying Hand Grab

Praying hand grab	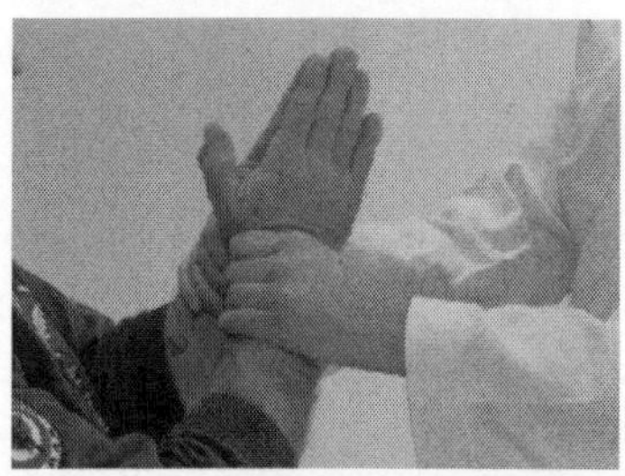
Step forward and strike the attacker's shoulder with a palm heal strike.	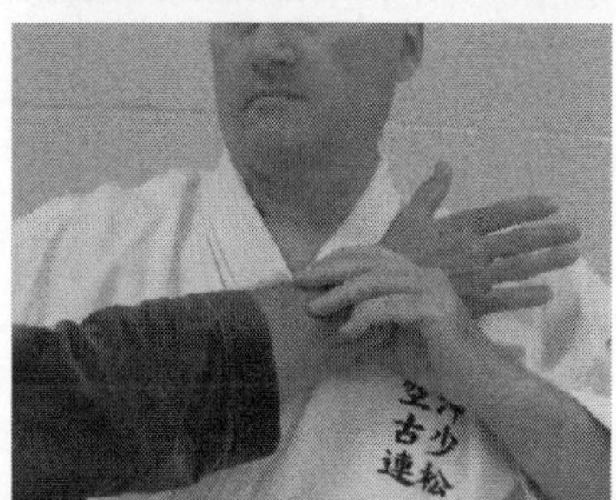

At the same time compress a wrist lock and neck pressure point.	
Using your striking hand press your fingertip into the attacker's neck pressure point just below the ear.	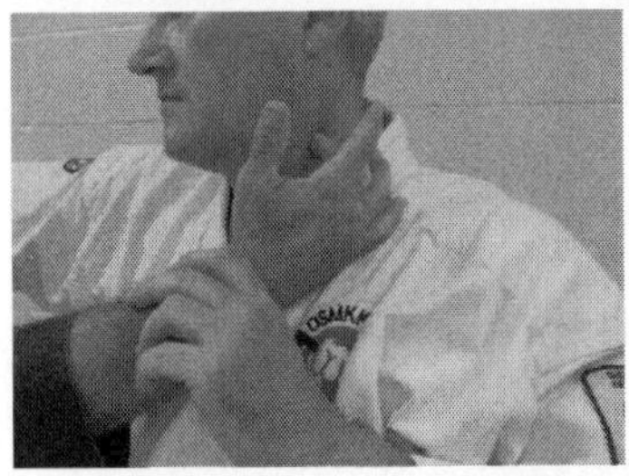
With your other hand slip your hand on top of the attacker's hand into a wrist lock using the base of your hand to put pressure on the back of their hand. *Note: The wrist lock can also be at the belt level.*	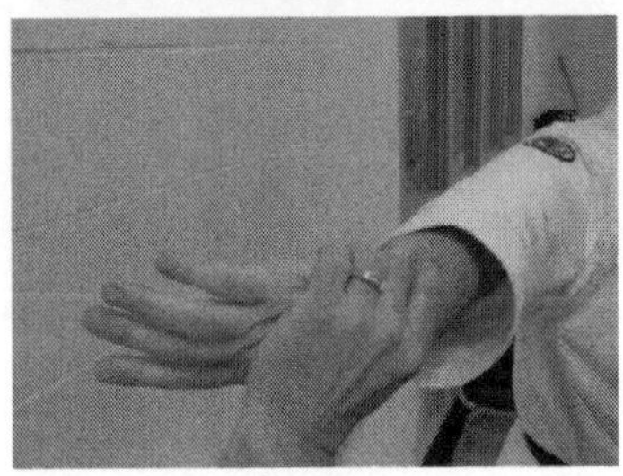

6-5 - Double Wrist Grab

Double wrist grab	

Turn one of your hands, so your palm is up.	
With your other hand, reach under the attacker's hand grabbing with a wrist out grab and your thumb on the back of their hand between the middle and ring fingers.	
Change body and without losing contact with your hand, roll your hand over and grab their fingers.	
Change body and use a wrist out technique to do a take down into an armbar with your knee against the back of the attacker's elbow and your foot is under their shoulderblade.	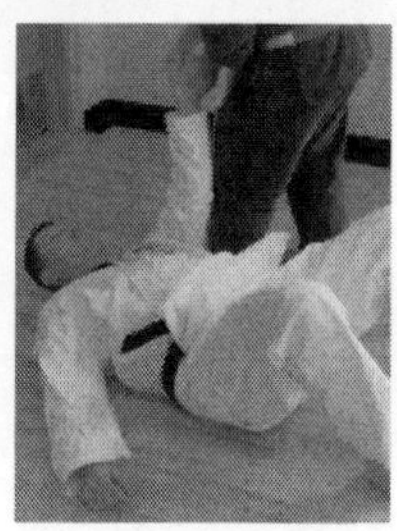

6-6 - Same Side Wrist Grab

Same side wrist grab	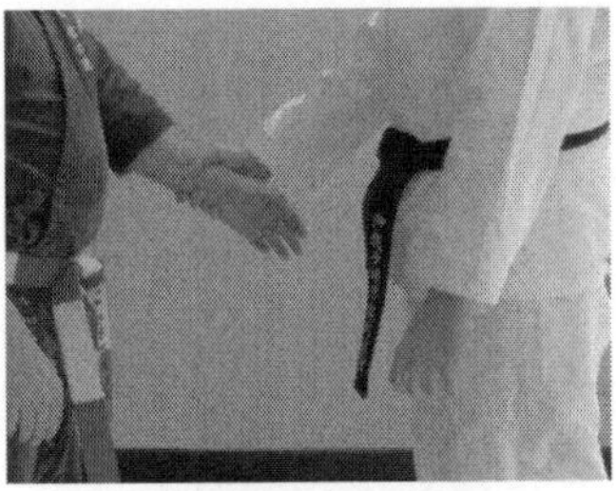
Change body and bring your hand up to shoulder high in front of you and with the hand that was grabbed, apply outward pressure and escape from the attacker.	
Using your other hand, grab the attacker's arm just behind where the attacker grabbed you.	
With your now free arm, use your elbow and strike the attacker's ribs.	

With the same hand strike to the attacker's groin and…	
then uppercut punch to the chin.	
Turning your body to face the same way, put their elbow on your shoulder and pull down into an armbar. *Note: Be very careful when practicing the armbar as it's very easy to hyperextend the elbow.*	

6-7 - Same Side Wrist Grab

Same side wrist grab	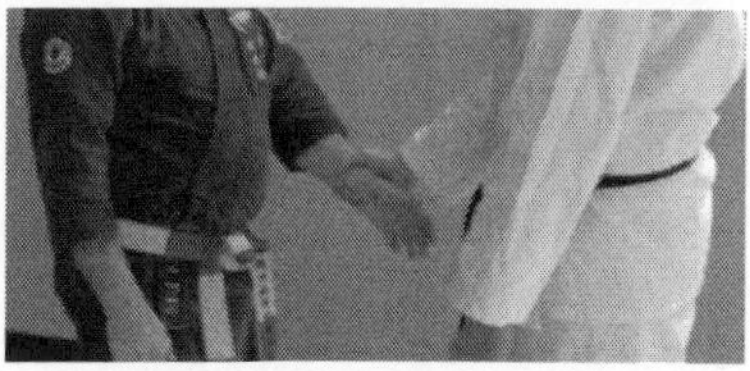

At the same time: Change body and grab the top of the attacker's hand.	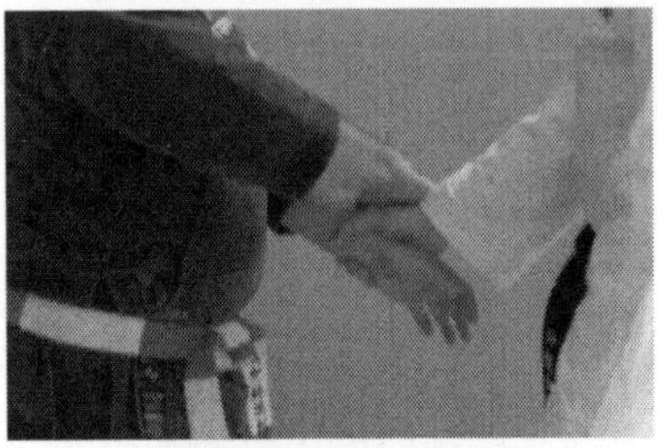
Open your grabbed hand going underneath and to the outside of the attacker.	
Continue to circle the hand over the top of the attacker's hand with your thumb up. This forms a "gooseneck" lock.	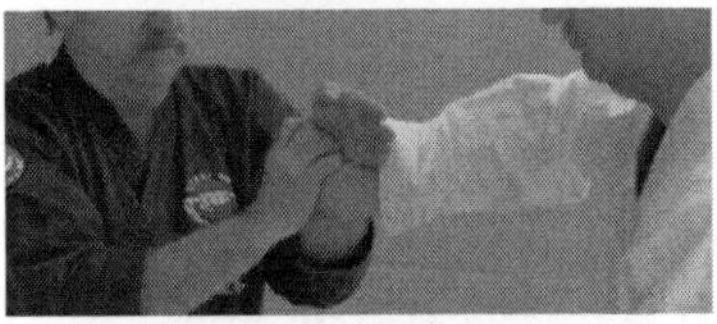
Keeping fingers together, press the bottom edge of your hand against attacker's wrist and down.	
Note: This is a close look at the "gooseneck" lock. Notice the 90 degree angle of the the wrist and elbow.	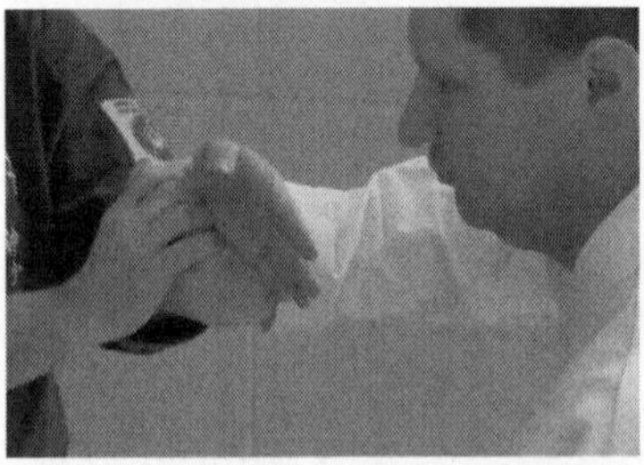

6-8 - Cross Hand Grab

Cross hand grab	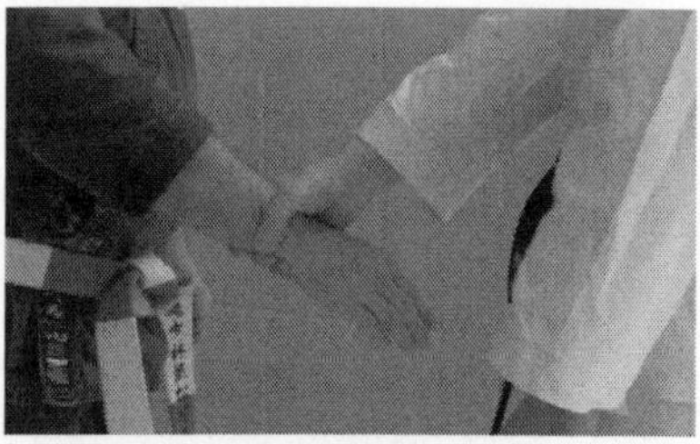
Grab the top of the attacker's hand.	
At the same time: Change body and make a fist with your grabbed hand, going underneath and to the outside of the attacker.	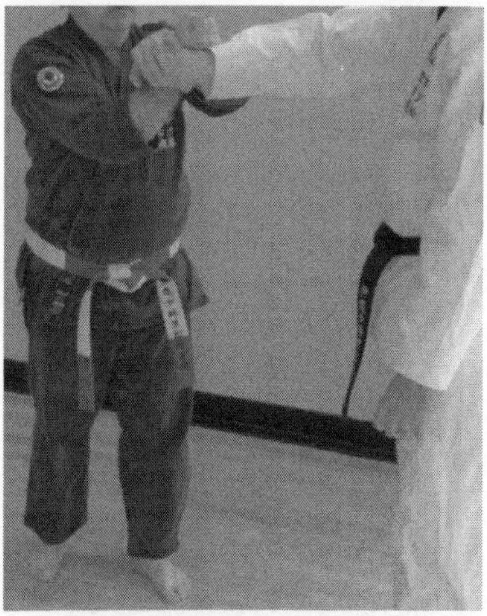
Continue to circle your fist over the top of the attacker's hand with your knuckles down.	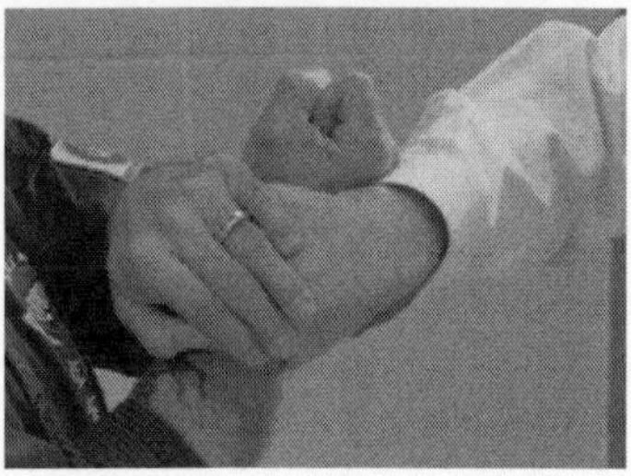

Using your first knuckle, apply downward pressure to the attacker's wrist bone and pull slightly toward your body.	
Note: Sometimes getting your knuckles all the way over can be a little hard. If this happens you can use the base of your fist or...	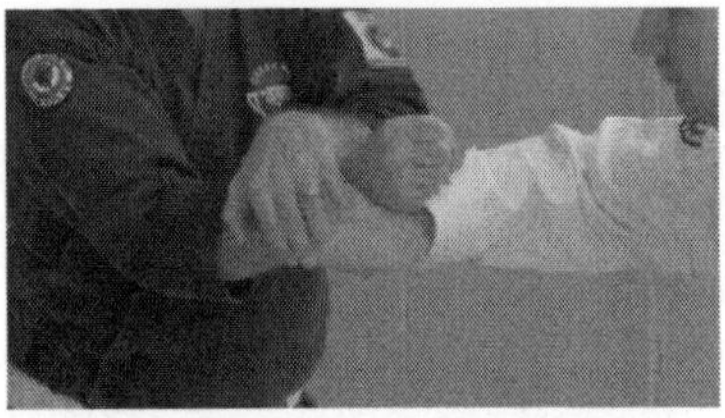
You can open your hand and grab the attacker's wrist.	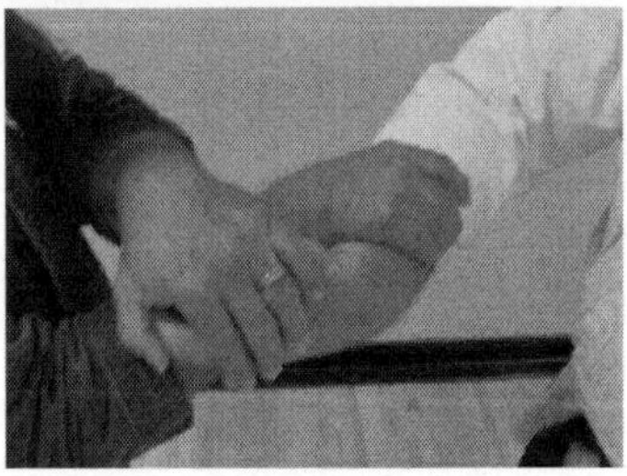

6-9 - Elbow Grab And Hook Punch

Same side elbow grab and roundhouse punch	

With your free hand strike the attacker's bicep hard with a knife hand strike.	
With the grabbed hand, go underneath and on top to grab the attacker's arm. Continue shooting your other arm close the attacker's neck.	
Wrap your arm and grab behind the attacker's head. Turn and step in close with your hip against the attacker's pelvis.	

Do a hip throw and throwing the attacker to the ground, pull down with the hand that is holding the attacker's arm.	
Maintain your hold on the attacker's arm and lift up on the attacker's arm and slip your foot under the attacker's shoulder and execute an arm bar.	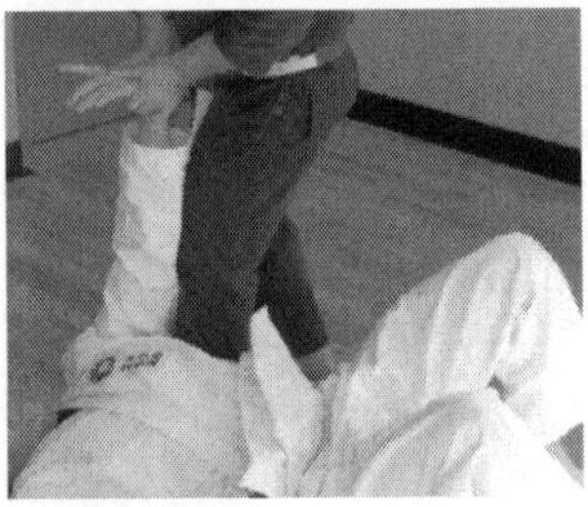

6-10 - Cross Elbow Grab

Cross elbow grab	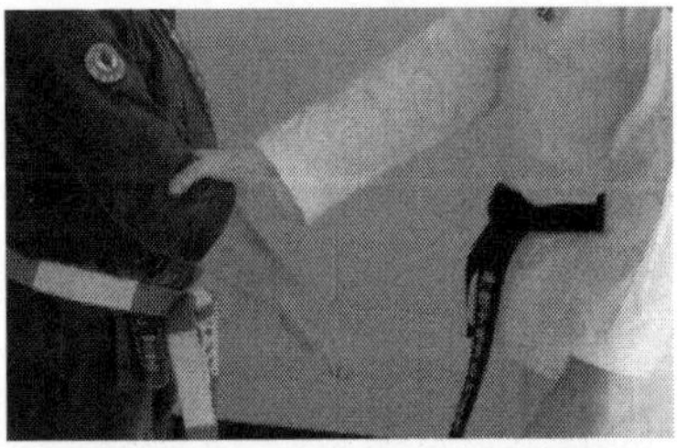
At the same time: Change body and grab the attacker's hand with your opposite hand.	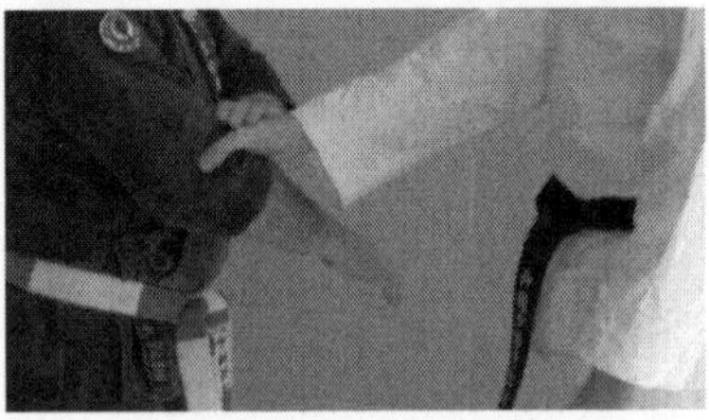

Stepping forward just a bit, bring your grabbed arm to the inside and over the top of the attacker's arm forming a gooseneck.	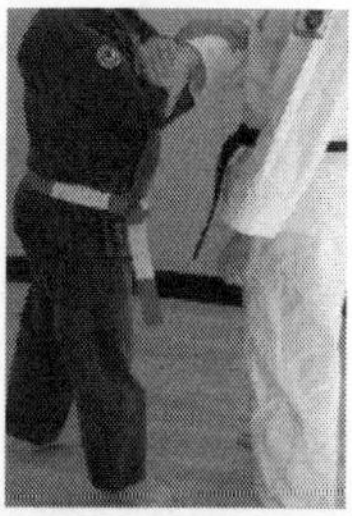
Using your fingers, grab the inside muscle, just below the elbow, of the attacker and apply a squeezing pressure. With a big step back lower the attacker to the ground.	

Chapter 12 - 5th Kyu Tuite

5-1 - Double Hand Grab To One Wrist

Double hand grab to one wrist	
Change body, so you're facing a 90 dregree angle to the attacker's outside and...	
Bring both your hands up and against the attacker's arm with your palms facing together.	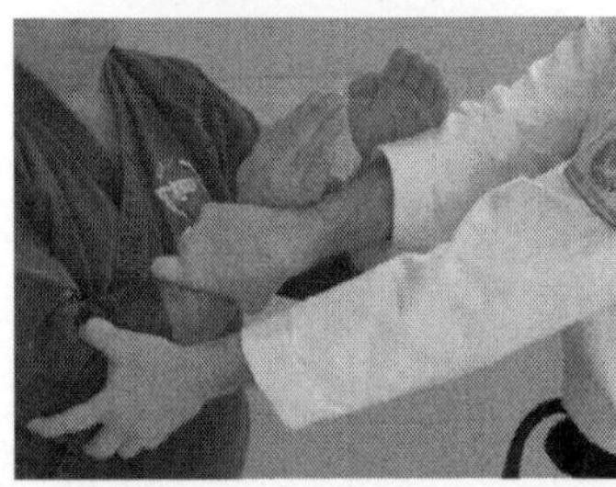
Push both your hands away from your body escaping from the hold.	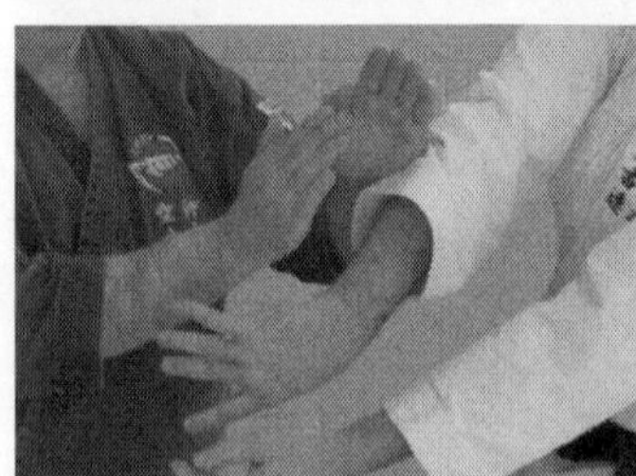

An option to this technique is to hold on to the attacker's wrist and use an arm bar for a take down.	

5-2 - One Hand Lapel Grab

One hand lapel grab	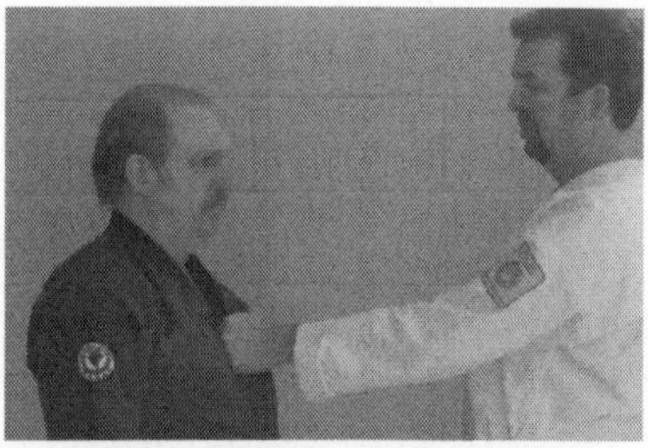
At the same time: With your same side hand, reach on top of the attacker's hand and compress their thumb and with your other hand reach under and grab the attacker's arm and push up causing the attacker's wrist to bend. *Note: both of your palms should be facing away from you and your thumbs pointing at each other.*	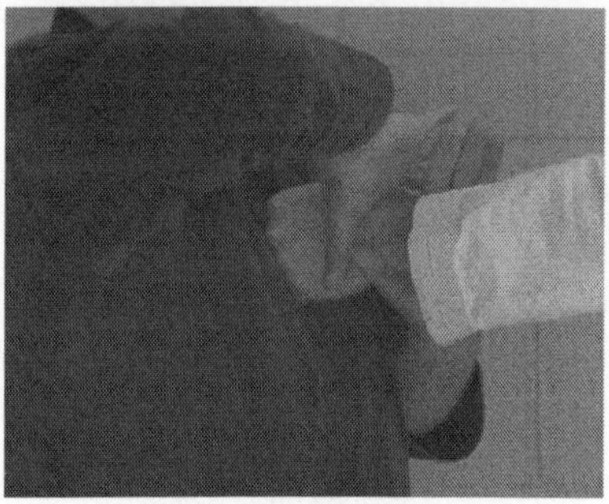
Change body and do a wrist out.	

Note the position of the hands on the attacker's hand.	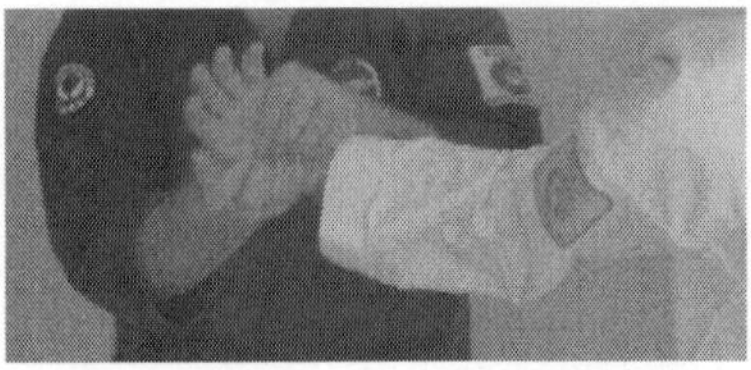

5-3 - One Hand Lapel Grab

One hand lapel grab	
At the same time: With your opposite side hand, reach on top of the attacker's hand, compressing their thumb and with your other hand reach under and grab the attacker's arm and push up causing the attacker's wrist to bend.	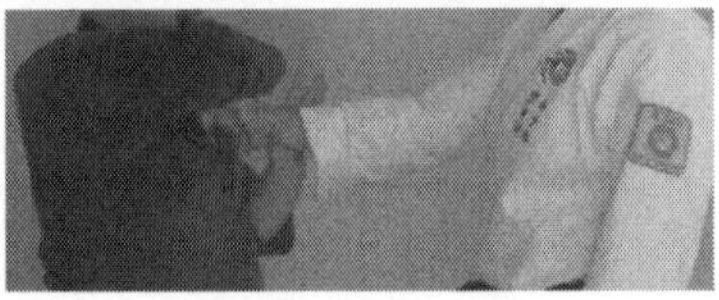
Change body and using your arm that is on the top, put your elbow completely on top of the attacker's arm …	
…forcing their arm down into an arm bar.	

5-4 - Double Hand Lapel Grab, One Hand Above

Double hand lapel grab with one hand above the other	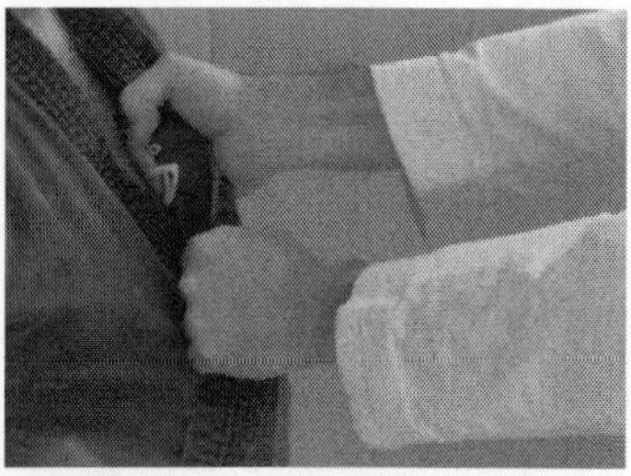
At the same time: With your same side hand as the attacker's lower hand, reach on top of the attacker's lower hand and compress their thumb and with your other hand reach under and grab the attacker's arm and push up causing the attacker's wrist to bend.	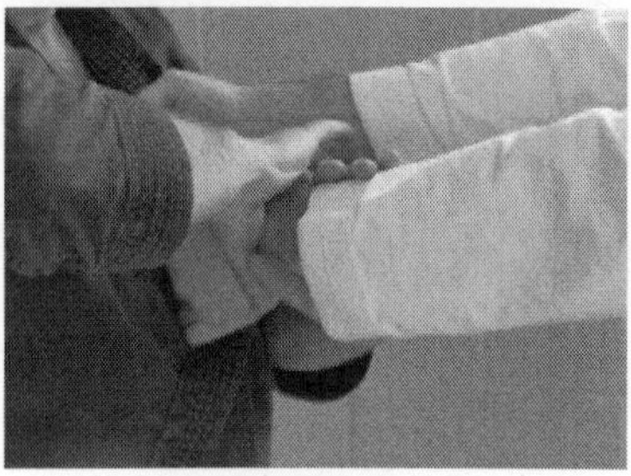
Change body and do a wrist out and at the same time using your elbow, break the attacker's hold with the other hand.	

5-5 - Wrist Grab And Punch

Wrist grab and punch	
With your free hand strike the attacker's bicep hard with a knife hand strike.	
At the same time: With the same hand, use a finger strike to the pressure points on the attacker's neck and…	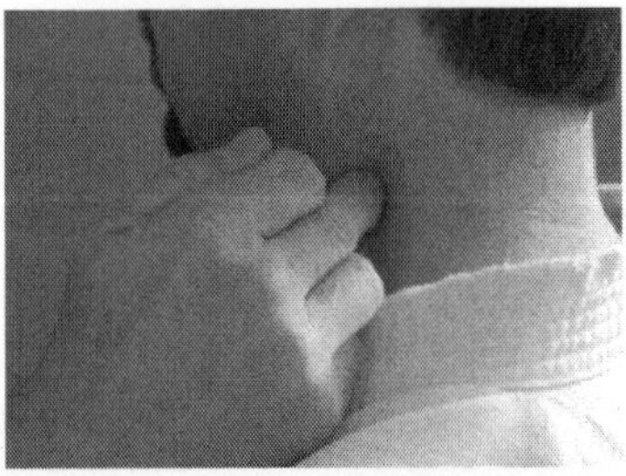
going to the outside, bring your grabbed arm underneath and grab the attacker's shirt or wrist.	

Change body and throw the attacker to the ground by pushing on their neck and pulling down on their arm, maintaining your hold on their shirt or wrist.	
At the same time: Put your foot nearest their head under their shoulder and pull up on their arm and against your knee creating an arm bar.	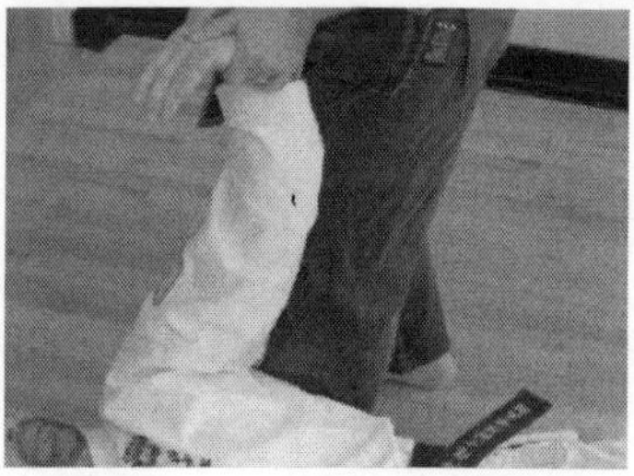

Chapter 13 - 4th Kyu Tuite

4-1 - Same Side Shoulder Grab

Same side shoulder grab	
At the same time: With your opposite side hand, reach on top of the attacker's hand, compressing their thumb and with your other hand reach under and grab the attacker's arm and push up causing the attacker's wrist to bend.	
Change body and using your arm that is on the top, put your elbow completely on top of the attacker's arm forcing their arm down into an arm bar.	

Shuffle forward and force their arm and body down toward the ground *Note: Remember to stay upright and don't lean over..*	
Once the attacker is face down on the floor drop on one knee on their shoulder joint and use your other knee as a fulcrum to put their arm in an armbar.	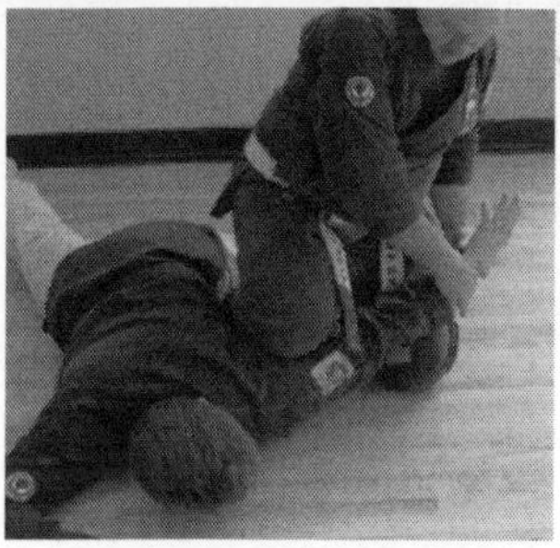

4-2 - Same Side Shoulder Grab

Same side shoulder grab	
With your same side hand, reach on top of the attacker's hand and compress their thumb and with your opposite hand reach under and grab the attacker's arm and push up causing the attacker's wrist to bend.	

Change body and do a wrist out.	
Bring the attacker down and to the floor.	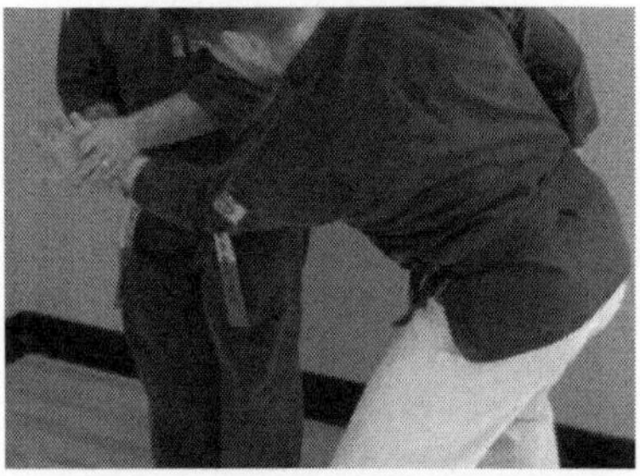
With your foot under the attacker's back and keeping presure on their wrist, apply a bent elbow armbar.	

4-3 - Elbow Grab And Hook Punch

Elbow grab and hook punch With your free hand strike the attacker's bicep hard with a knife hand strike.	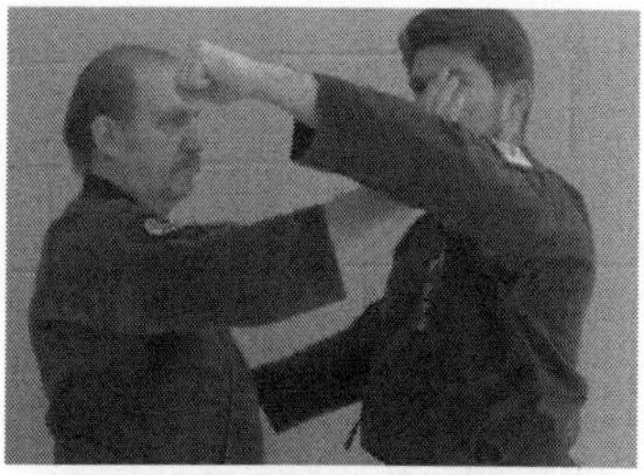
With the same hand strike the attacker's temple with a single knuckle punch.	
At the same time: Stepping in and so you're facing the same way as the attacker, keep their arm bent and with the arm that was grabbed, go to the inside and loop over trapping the attacker's arm with your arm and behind your back by keeping your arm close to your body.	
Use your free hand to press against the attacker's chest adding more pressure to their shoulder. You can add additional pressure by grabbing your own hand that is pressing against the attacker. *Note: It's very important to keep the attacker's arm bent and close to your body.*	

4-4 - Elbow Grab And Hook Punch

Elbow grab and hook punch With your free hand strike the attacker's bicep hard with a knife hand strike.	
With the same hand strike the attacker's neck with a knife hand strike and with your grabbed hand, go to the inside and underneath and grab the attacker's elbow or sleeve.	
Grab the back of the attacker's head, change body and pulling the attacker's arm down throw them to the floor an their back maintaining your hold on the attacker's arm and land your knee on the attacker's shoulder joint and the other one on the floor. Keep your knees close together and with the attacker's elbow against your knee that's on the floor, pull down in an arm bar.	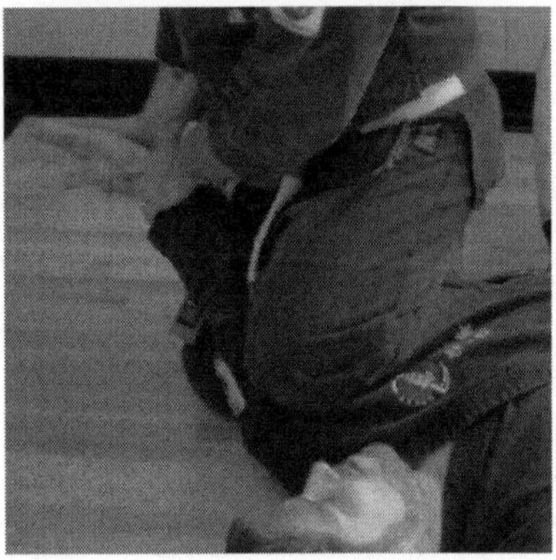
Note: Keep in mind that when you land on the attacker's shoulder, both knees are coming down at the same time with all your weight. The attacker's shoulder will cushion your or landing. *Warning: Be VERY careful practicing this part of the technique!*	

4-5 - Elbow Grab And Hook Punch

Elbow grab and hook punch With your free hand strike the attacker's bicep hard with a knife hand strike.	
With the arm that was grabbed go to the outside and over the top of the attacker's arm and...	
Grab the attacker's gi or shirt.	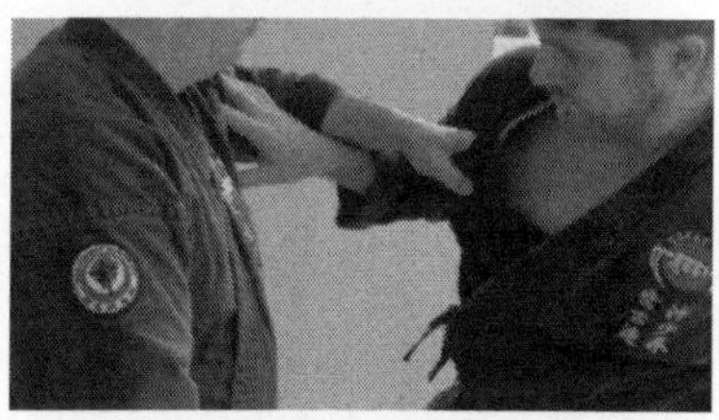
Grab the attacker's head with your free hand and pulling the attacker's gi down, throw them to the floor on their back. With the hand that was on their head, punch to the attacker's face.	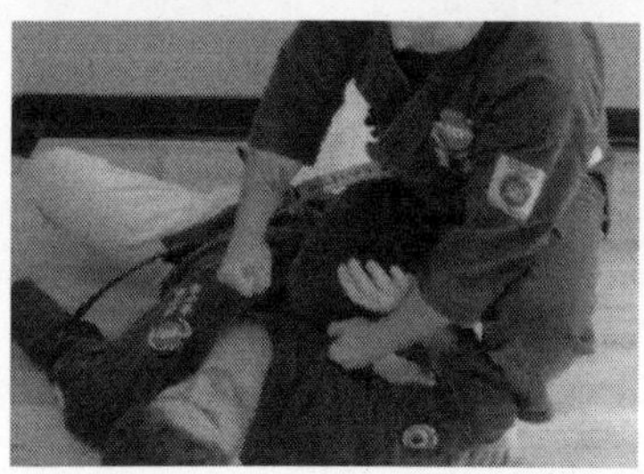

Chapter 14 - 3rd Kyu Tuite

3-1 - Praying Hand Grab

Praying hand grab	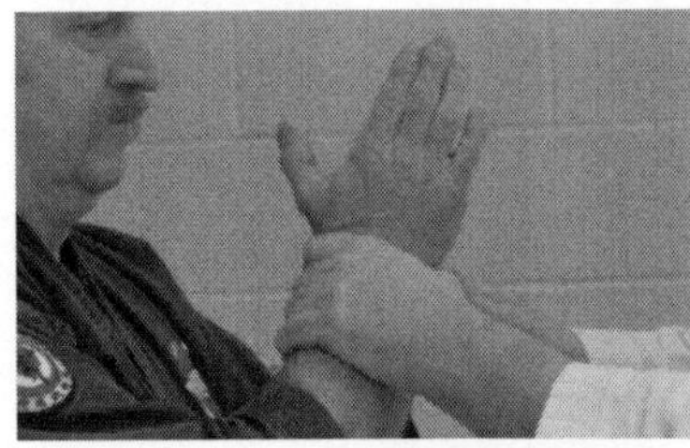
Step forward and strike the attacker's shoulder with a palm heal strike.	
With your other hand slip your hand on top of and grab the attacker's wrist.	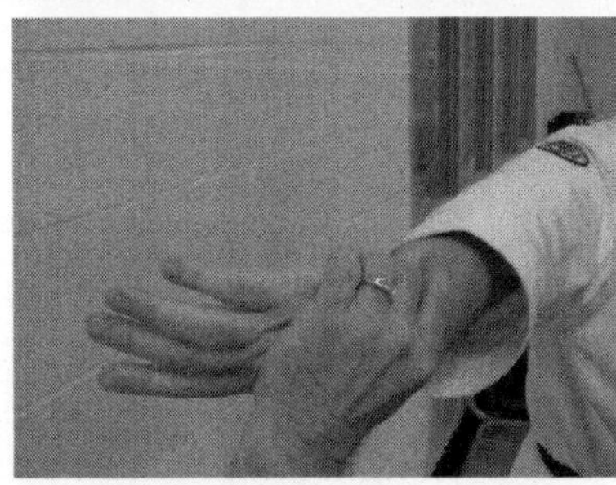
With the other hand reach over and exchange your hands, using a wrist lock on the attacker.	

Step around, so you're facing the same way as the attacker and with your, now free hand, use the base of that hand against the attacker's elbow into an arm bar.	
Force the attacker to the floor face first and land your knee on the attacker's tricept and the other one on the floor.	
With the attacker's elbow pointed up, pull up on the attacker's hand.	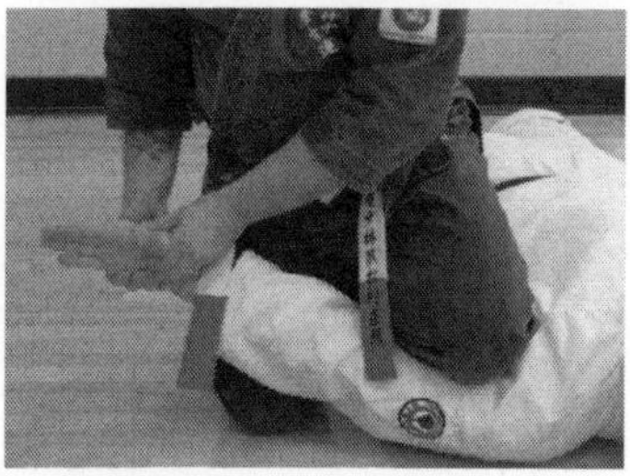

3-2 - Wrist Grab And Hook Punch

Wrist Grab and hook punch With your free hand strike the attacker's bicep hard with a knife hand strike.	

With the same hand do an eye jab and scraping your fingers across both the attacker's eyes.	
Bring your palm up, so you're looking at your own palm solar plexus high.	
With your free hand reach under the attacker's hand grabbing with a wrist out grab and your thumb in the back of their hand.	
Change body and use a wrist out technique to do a take down, landing the attacker on their back.	
Keeping the attacker's elbow bent, keep the wrist out turn levering their elbow against your knee.	

3-3 - Wrist Grab And Hook Punch

Wrist grab and hook punch With your free hand strike the attacker's bicep hard with a knife hand strike.	
With the same hand do an eye jab and scraping your fingers across both the attacker's eyes.	
Bring your palm up, so you're looking at your own palm solar plexus high.	
With your free hand reach under the attacker's hand grabbing with a wrist out grab and with your thumb in the back of their hand.	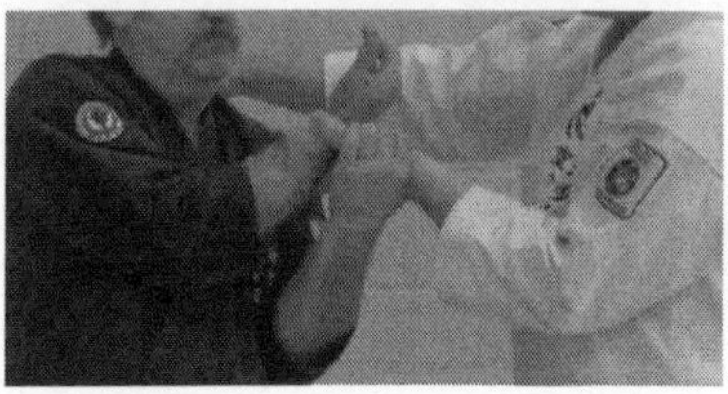

Change body and start with a wrist out technique.	
Free the arm that was grabbed and with the free hand grab the attacker's elbow and raise it up and back to make them fall backwards landing them onto their back.	
Maintaining the wrist lock, push the back of the attacker's hand onto the ground creating a goose neck.	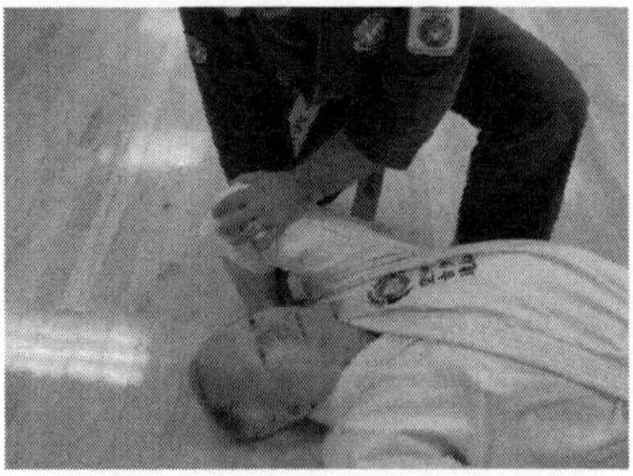
Maintain the pressure on the wrist and switch hands and punch the attacker's face.	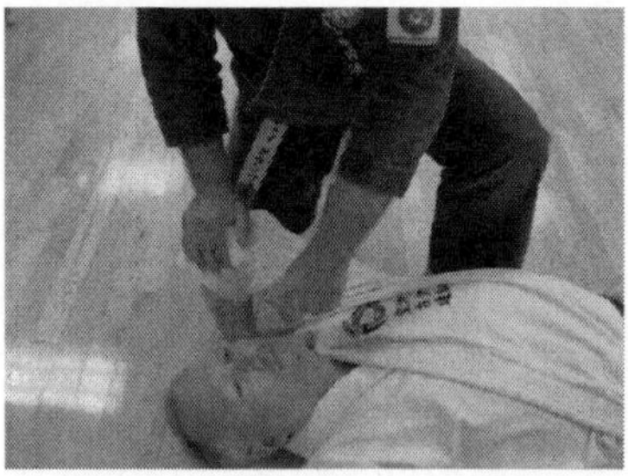

3-4 - Stepping Forward Punch

Stepping forward punch Change body and with the same side hand, block across and grab the attacker's hand with a wrist lock.	
Reinforce your hold on the attacker's hand with your other hand.	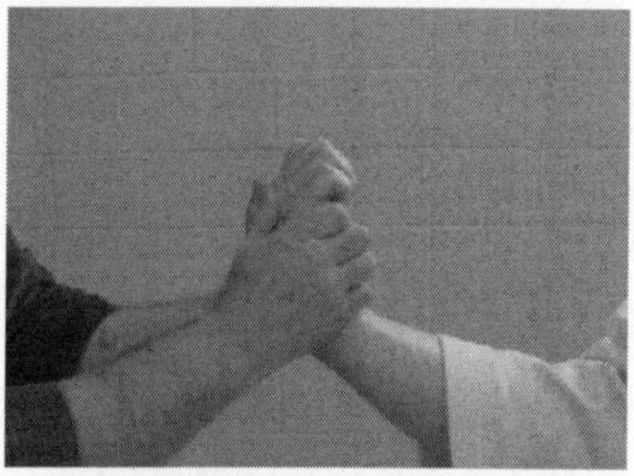
Change body again, but the opposite direction doing a wrist out and...	

Throwing the attacker to the ground and maintaining the wrist lock with both hands.	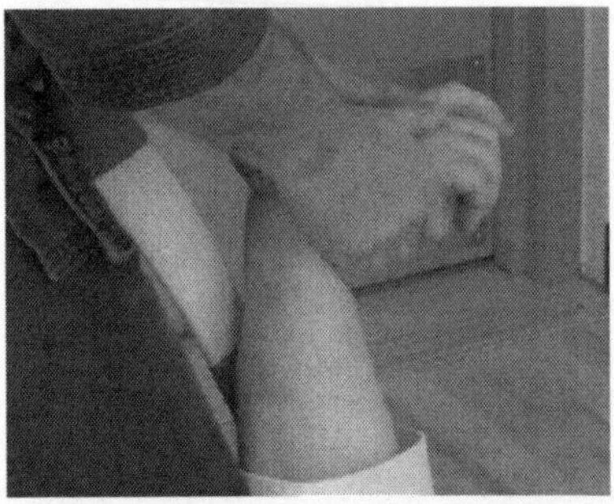
Put your foot under the attacker's shoulder and lever the attacker's elbow against your knee, pulling up at the same time and twisting the wrist out.	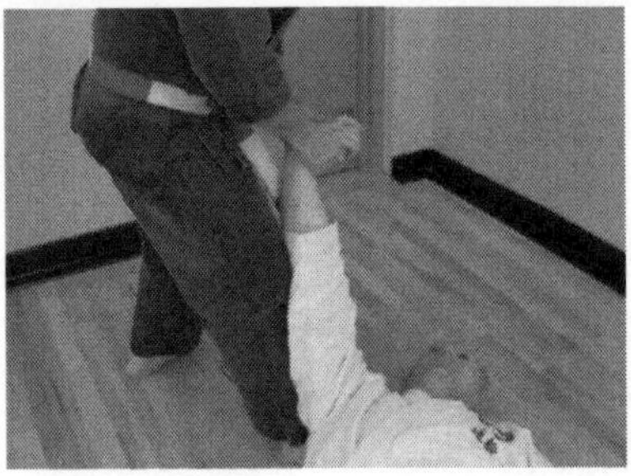

3-5 - Wrist Grab And Hook Punch

Wrist grab and hook punch With your free hand strike the attacker's bicep hard with a knife hand strike.	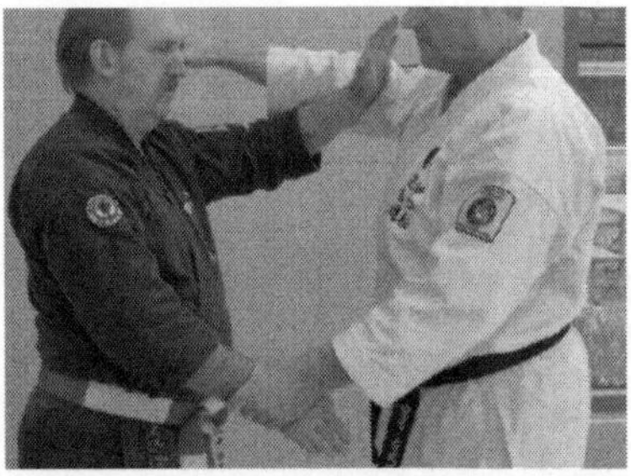
With the same hand do an eye jab and scraping your fingers across both the attacker's eyes.	

With the same hand grab the attacker's wrist and...	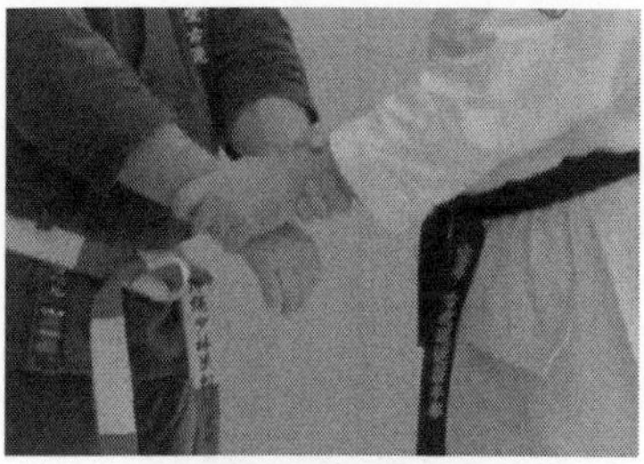
Pull their arm up maintaining your hold on the attacker's wrist and step under the attacker's raised arm turning,	
ending up behind the attacker creating an arm lock behind them.	

With your free hand, use a claw hand to the front of the attacker's throat.	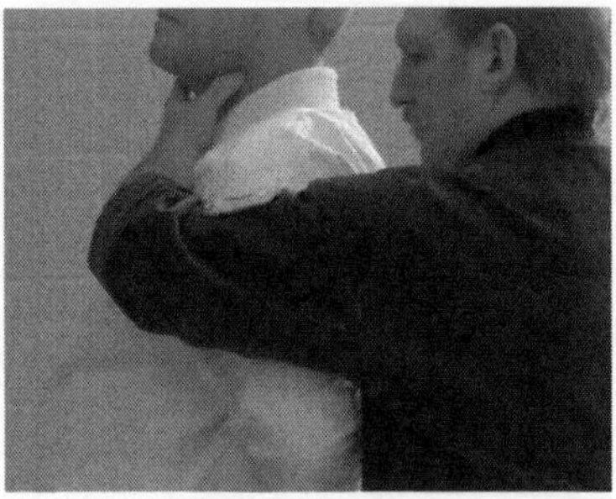
Finish with a kick to back of the attacker's knee causing them to fall down and at the same time pulling up with your claw hand on their throat.	

Chapter 15 - 2nd Kyu Tuite

2-1 - Elbow Grab And Hook Punch

Elbow grab and hook punch With your free hand strike the attacker's bicep hard with a knife hand strike.	
With the same hand strike the attacker's neck with a knife hand strike.	
At the same time: With the same hand grab the attacker's hand that grabbed your elbow and...	
Step forward and with your grabbed arm loop your hand, going to the outside, over the attacker's arm using the base of your hand to bend the attacker's elbow.	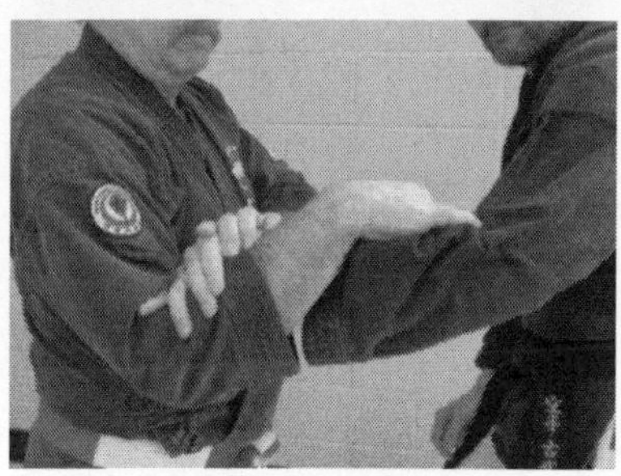

With the same hand going to the outside and grabbing underneath the attacker's elbow, pull the attacker down onto their back.	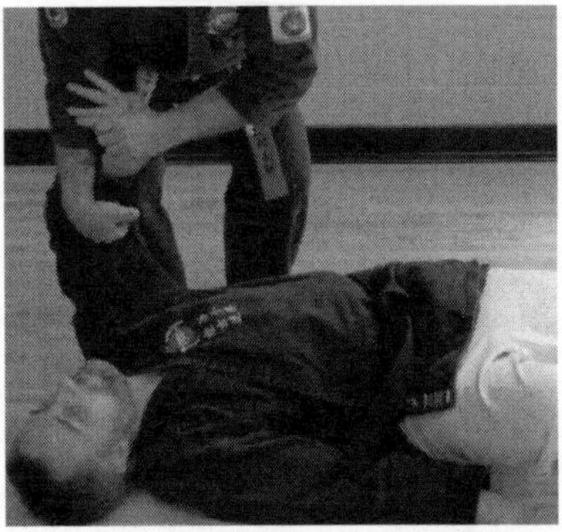
Keep the attacker's arm bent in a goose neck applying pressure with both hands and using your knee as a fulcrum.	

2-2 - Wrist Grab And Hook Punch

Wrist grab and hook punch With your free hand strike the attacker's bicep hard with a knife hand strike.	

With the same hand do an eye jab and scraping your fingers across both the attacker's eyes.	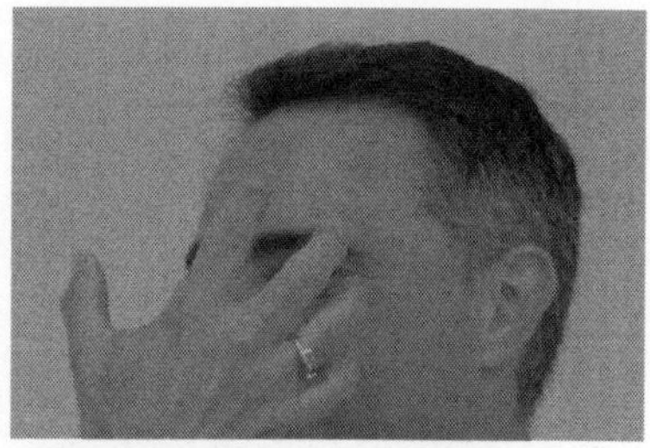
At the same time: Change body and with the same hand, grab the attacker's wrist of the hand that grabbed your wrist and...	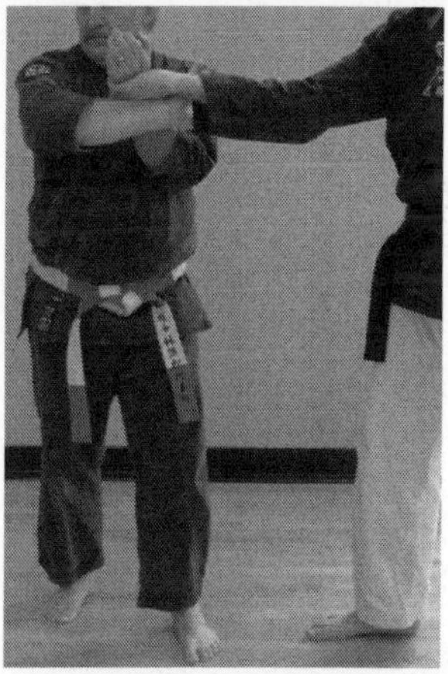
Step forward stepping between the attacker's legs and lifting up on the attacker's arm, drop down on the knee that is away from the attacker and do an elbow strike to the attacker's groin.	

At the same time: With the striking arm grab the attacker's leg or pants and pulling up...	
Rotating to the outside and bring the attacker's arm over your head, switching knees, throwing the attacker across your back and down in front of you.	
Keep the attacker's elbow bent and apply pressure useing your knee, as a fulcrum.	

2-3 - Wrist Grab And Hook Punch

Wrist grab and hook punch With your free hand strike the attacker's bicep hard with a knife hand strike.	
With the same hand do an eye jab and scraping your fingers across both the attacker's eyes.	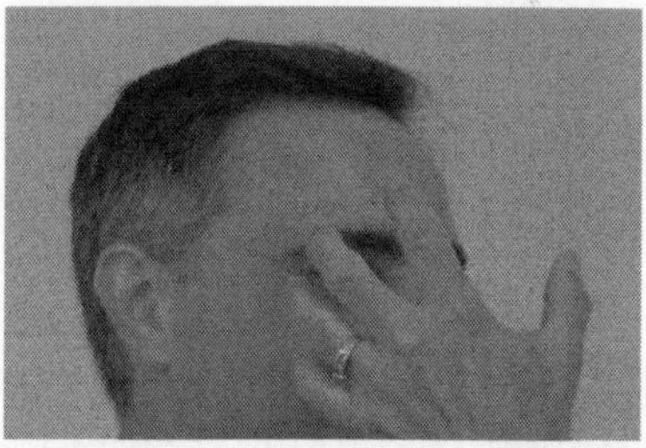
With the same hand grab the attacker's wrist of the hand that grabbed your wrist.	

Lifting the attacker's arm up and maintaining your grip, turn counterclockwise all the way around (360 degrees).	
Support the attacker's elbow with your other hand and force the attacker's arm back and to the ground.	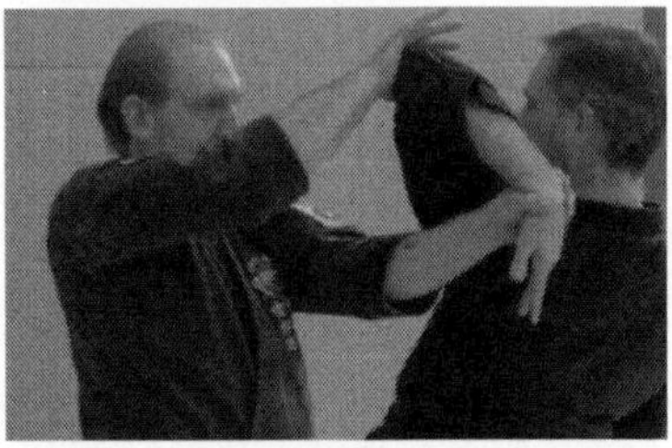
Press the back of the attacker's wrist to the ground and…	
switch hands. Finish with a punch to the attacker's face.	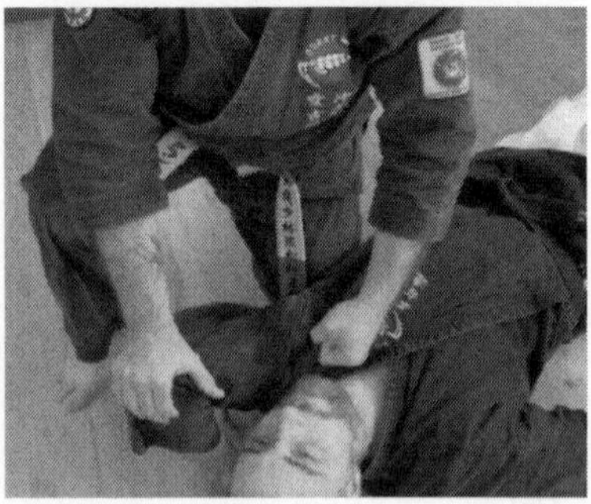

2-4 - One Hand Lapel Grab

One hand lapel grab	
At the same time: Change body and with your opposite side hand as the attacker, grab the attacker's hand that grabbed you. With your same side hand strike under the attacker's upper arm that grabbed you with a ridge hand.	
With the same hand reach over and change hands to grab the attacker's hand at the base of the thumb and into a wrist out turn.	
Change body and with your free hand strike the attacker's ear with an open hand.	

With the same hand grab the attacker's neck, step around and throw the attacker to the ground on their back.	
Maintain your wrist lock and drop one knee onto the attacker's shoulder joint and use your other knee as a flocrum for an arm bar, turning the wrist out for added pressure.	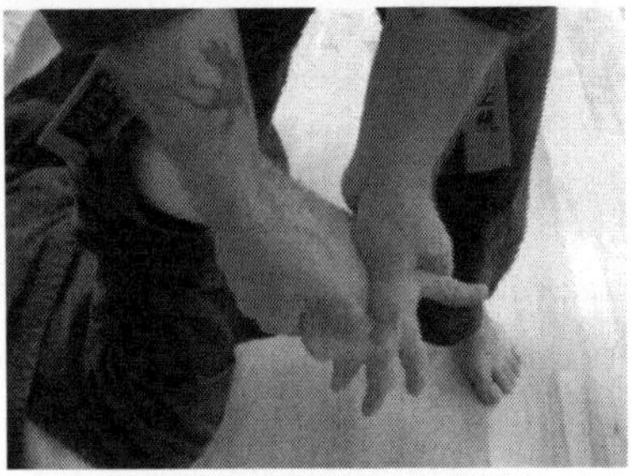

2-5 - Two Hand Choke

Attacker steps forward and reaches for a two hand choke	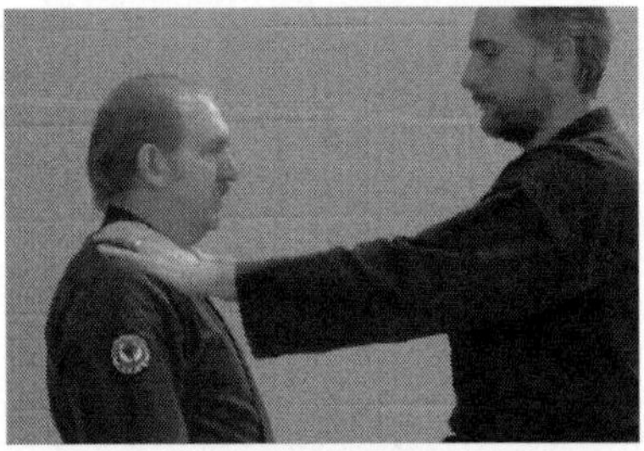
At the same time: Step forward and grab the attacker's belt or pants and...	

Do a finger srike to the soft base of the throat, just above the collar bone, with a finger tip strike.	
Note: This should be a push/pull action with the fingertip pushing and the other hand pulling the belt.	

Chapter 16 - 1st Kyu Tuite

1-1 - Cross Wrist Grab

Cross wrist grab	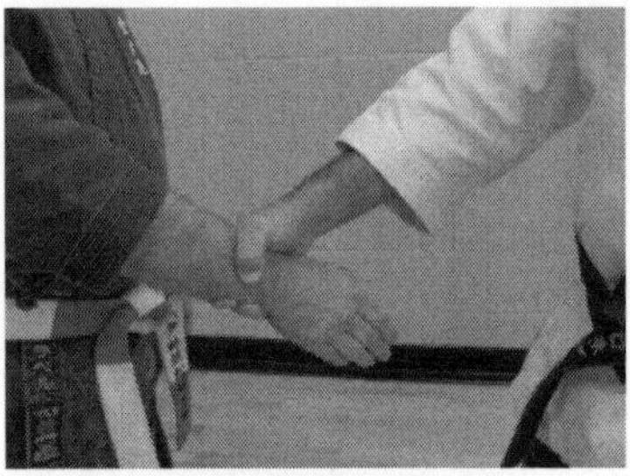
With your free hand grab the top of the attacker's hand that grabbed you wrist.	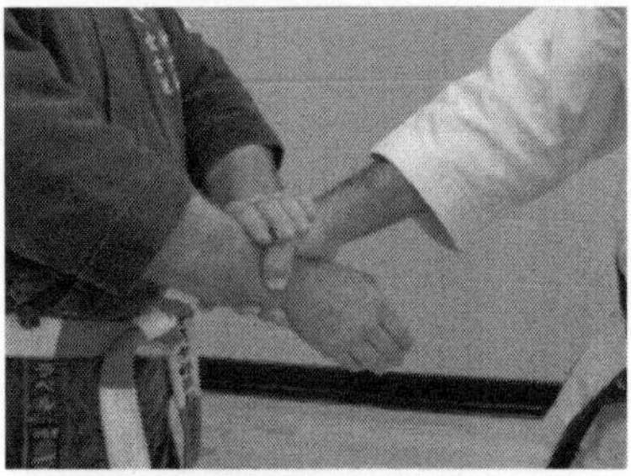
Step forward to bend the attacker's elbow.	

With the hand that was grabbed loop it to the outside and over the top grabbing the attacker's wrist creating a goose neck.	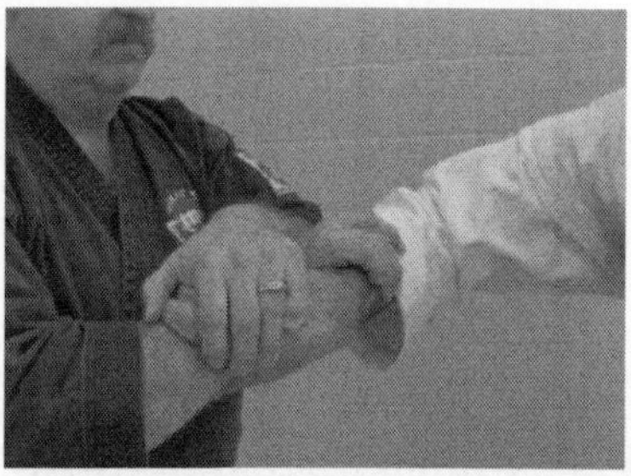
Maintain the goose neck and step back bringing the attacker face down into the ground.	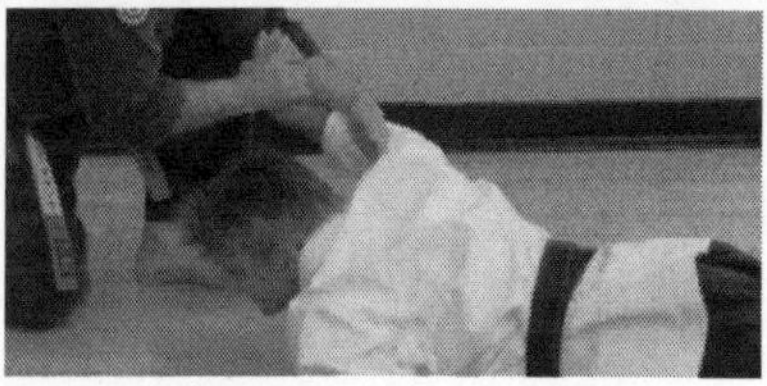

1-2 - Same Side Elbow Grab

Same side elbow grab	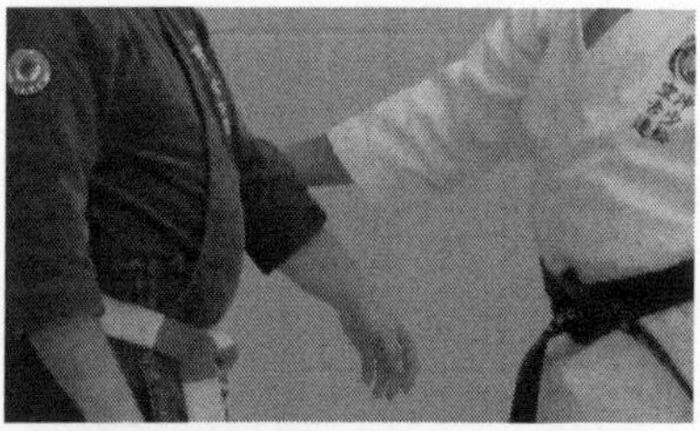
With your free hand grab the top of the attacker's hand that grabbed your wrist.	
At the same time: Stepping into the attacker, and with the hand of the arm that was grabbed and going to the outside, loop over the attacker's arm and using the base of your hand, bend the attacker's arm creating a goose neck.	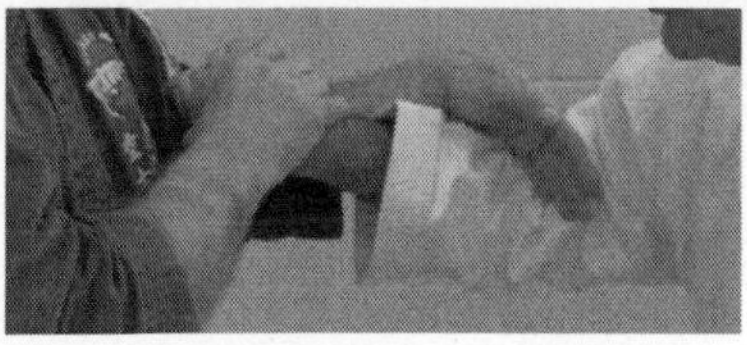

Maintain the goose neck and step back bringing the attacker face down into the ground.	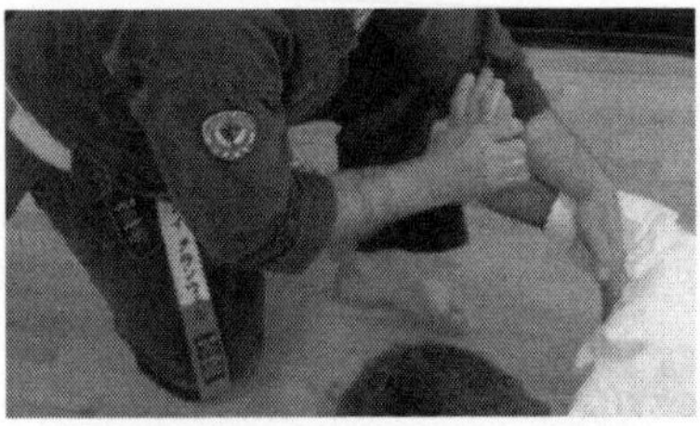

1-3 - Same Side Lapel Grab

Same side lapel grab	
With your opposite side hand, grab the top of the attacker's hand that grabbed you.	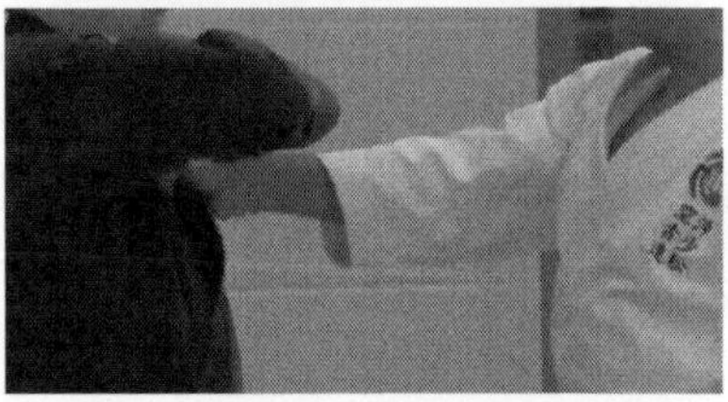
At the same time: Stepping into the attacker, and...	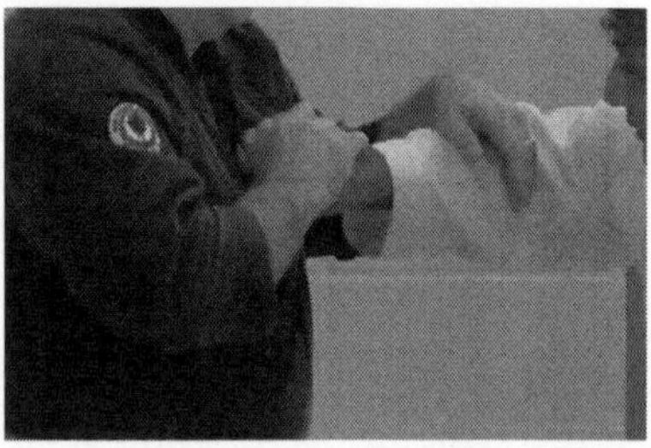

With your free hand loop over the attacker's arm, going to the outside and using the base of your hand, bend the attacker's arm creating a goose neck.	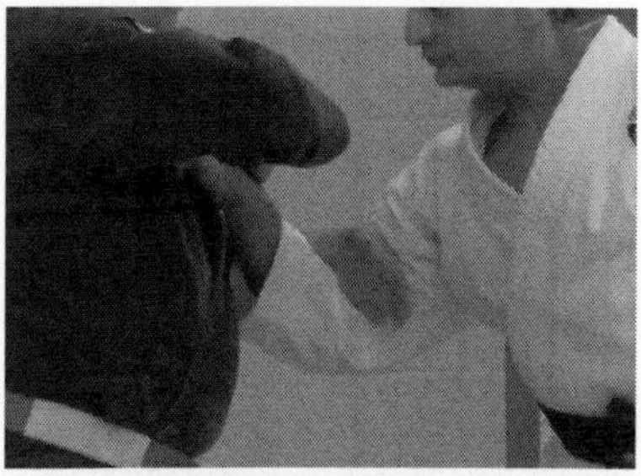
Maintain the goose neck and step back bringing the attacker face down into the ground.	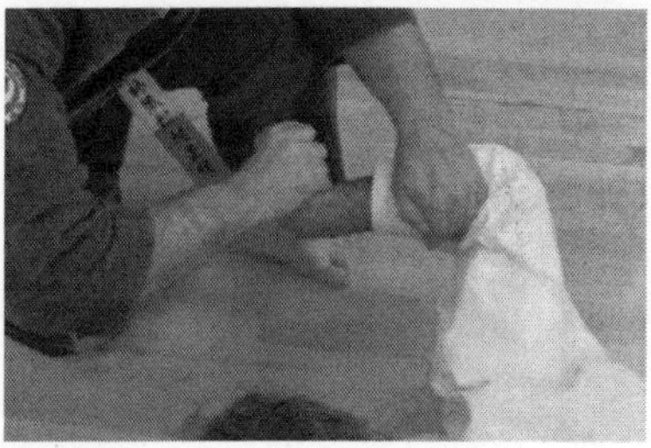

1-4 - Same Side Shoulder Grab

Same side shoulder grab	
With your opposite side hand, grab the top of the attacker's hand that grabbed you.	

At the same time: With your free hand loop over the attacker's arm, going to the outside and Using the base of your hand, bend the attacker's arm creating a goose neck. *Note: Since you don't step into the attacker, their arm will not be bent much and they will be bending over slightly.*	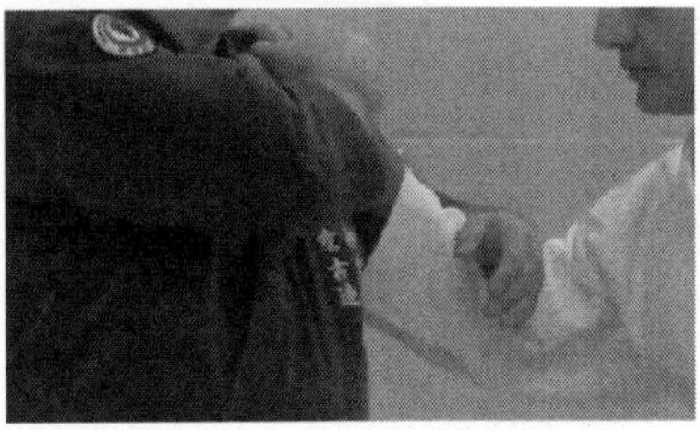
Maintain the goose neck on the attacker's wrist and with your free hand reach underneath and grab the back of the attacker's head.	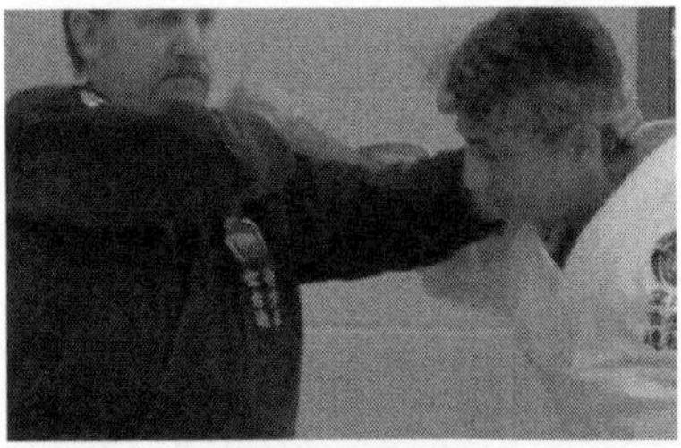
Pull the attacker's head under their arm bringing them to the ground on their back.	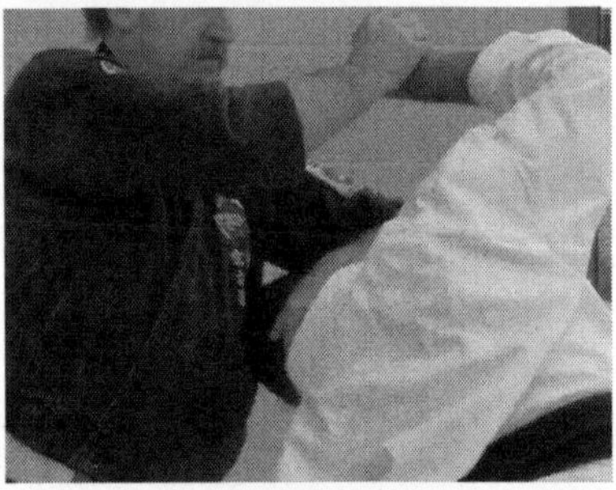
Slip your foot under the attacker's shoulder and lever the attacker's elbow against your knee, pulling up at the same time and twisting the wrist out.	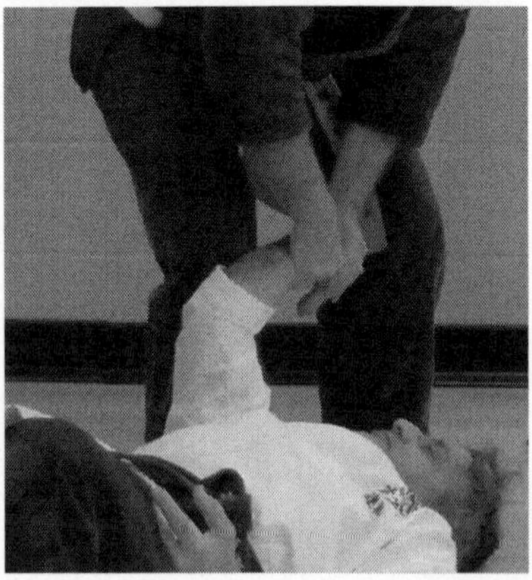

1-5 - Shaking Hands

Shaking hands	
With your opposite leg from the hand that is shaking, step into the attacker in front of their foot.	

At the same time: Turn your body 180 degrees, so you're facing the same way as the attacker and with your free hand reach over the top of the attacker's arm above their elbow wrapping your arm around theirs.	
With your other hand pull down on the attacker's fingers into an arm bar.	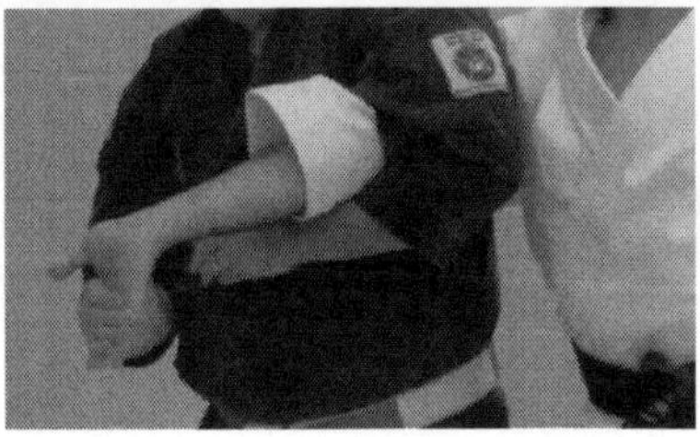

Maintain the arm bar with the arm that's wrapped around the attacker's arm and release the attacker's fingers At the same time: Lift the attacker's arm up to your should and turn facing the attacker and using your free hand, strike the attacker's groin with a palm heal strike.	
With the same hand, follow up with a claw strike to the attacker's throat.	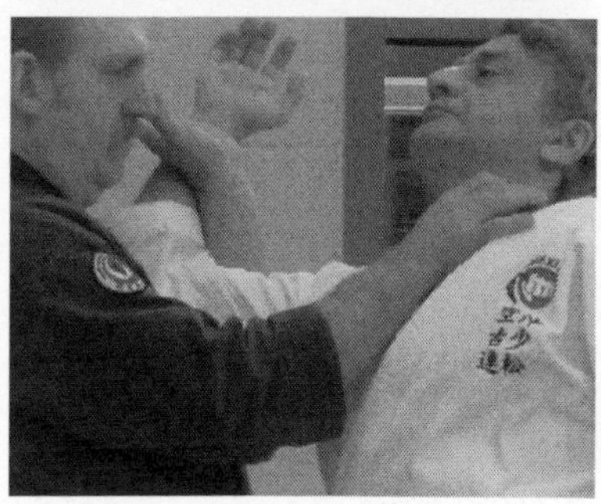

Kicking the attacker's leg, to bring them off balance, push their head back throwing them to the ground on their back.	
Maintain your hold and follow with a gound hold.	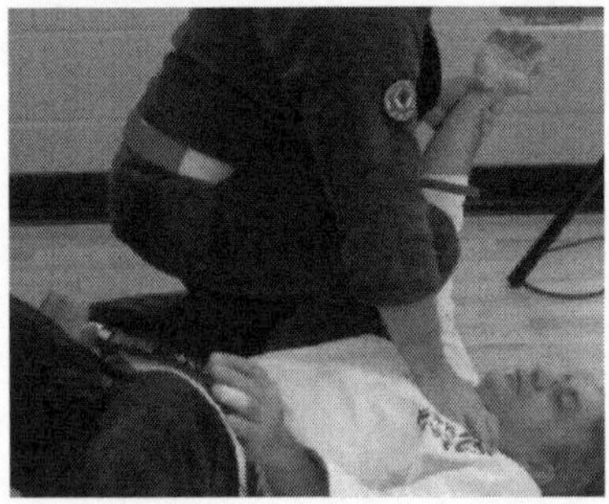

Chapter 17 - Summary/Conclusion

These sets of tuite will help you in practicing your tuite, but be ready to go from one tuite technique to another if the first one isn't working. The way to practice this is by studying how the joints work and learning flow drills to help you go from one technique to another.

There are three parts to our karate and tuite is only one part of it. To be effective in all aspects of karate it is very important to understand how all the parts fit together. The main goal of karate is to stay upright and not get into a grappling match on the ground. In the MMA ring you only have to worry about one opponent, but in the real world you never know whether the person you have on the ground has a buddy waiting to jump you. Always be aware of the second or even third attacker. Staying upright will give you the advantage.

If you do end up on the ground, do not forget all the tuite and joint locks will still work. There will be a new set of angles, but remember whether on the ground or standing upright, all the joints will always work the same. "It's all about body physics"!

Appendix A - Tuite Cheat Sheet

10 kyu

1. Same Side Single Hand – Over the hand and in.
2. Cross hand – Over the hand and in.
3. Double hand – both over the hand and in.
4. First 3 quick
5. Same side single hand – close, open and change body

9 Kyu

1. Same side wrist grab – palm up, roll down and push against fingers.
2. Elbow grab – grab wrist and push against fingers with elbow.
3. Shoulder grab – grab with opposite hand, use armpit.
4. Lapel grab – same side thumb lock and elbow pressure point.

8 Kyu

1. Same side wrist grab – kick, thumb lock, football technique
2. Elbow grab – kick, thumb lock slap up arm and shuto technique to elbow.
3. Shoulder grab – kick thumb lock, dislocate shoulder and slide in.
4. Reach for choke – whitecrane, strike to face.
5. Bear hug

7 Kyu

1. Buddy grab
2. Hair grab
3. Hand shake
4. Double lapel grab – grab over the top and use thumb locks.
5. Punch – shuto block and step all the way behind to arm bar.

6 Kyu

1. Reach for choke – grab both hands, with big circle turn hands over.
2. Reach for choke – grab both hands, step forward and turn hands over one at a time.
3. Praying hands – grab both hands and wrist locks and push at 45.
4. Praying hands - strike shoulder, grab other hand and neck poke.
5. Double wrist grab – palm up, wrist out
6. Same side wrist grab – palm up, sweep, elbow to ribs, down/up
7. Same side wrist grab – change body, other hand knife hand
8. Cross hand wrist grab – grab hand, over the top with fist
9. Wrist grab/punch – (knife hand to bicep) hip throw
10. Cross elbow grab – grab, over the top grab triceps

5 Kyu

1. 2 hand single wrist grab – underneath push with both knife hands
2. Lapel grab – wrist out
3. Lapel grab – wrist in, arm bar
4. Lapel grab 2 hands – wrist out on bottom hand
5. Wrist grab/punch – finger jab, grab on top and pull down

4 Kyu

1. Shoulder grab – wrist in, arm bar
2. Shoulder grab – wrist out
3. Elbow grab/punch – strike bicep, over the top, trap in bent position
4. Wrist grab/punch – finger jab, grab on top and pull down
5. Elbow grab/punch – strike bicep, over the top, grab lapel

3 Kyu

1. Praying hands – rake eyes, wrist in, arm bar with knife hand to ground
2. Wrist grab/punch – rake, palm up, wrist out, takedown
3. Wrist grab/punch – rake, palm up, bend elbow, switch hands, wrist out, takedown
4. Step punch – same side grab on top of hand, step back, wrist out
5. Wrist grab/punch – rake, grab wrist, pull up and walk through, switch hands, throat grab

2 Kyu

1. Elbow grab/punch – rake, grab top of hand, other hand over the top, under, pull down
2. Wrist grab/punch – rake, palm up, switch hands, go to knee, elbow groin, throw
3. Wrist grab/punch – rake, grab wrist, pull up and walk through counter clockwise, bend elbow to ground, trap, punch
4. Lapel grab – opposite hand grab, ridge hand under arm, cup ear, wrist out
5. Two hand choke reach – grab belt, finger to throat

1 Kyu

1. Cross wrist grab – under, over top, bend arm and pull to ground face down
2. Same side elbow grab – grab hand, over top, straight arm and pull to ground face down
3. Lapel grab - grab hand, over top, bend arm and pull to ground face down
4. Lapel grab - grab hand, over top, bend arm, go under, grab back of head, takedown
5. Hand shake – step in, over the top, arm bar, lift arm up, groin strike, throat grab, throw on back

Author - Biography

Jay Gravelle

Jay Gravelle is an accomplished trainer and public speaker, whose, varied professional background includes a number of teaching positions. A true "people person", Jay is well versed in adult and youth learning techniques and is an expert communicator and motivator as well. Students have the opportunity to learn from a professional who genuinely understands the challenges and demands in today's environment.

Jay has trained thousands of students both male and female, adult and youth in karate, self-defense, joint locks and weapons.

Jay's delivery style has been described as "knowledgeable", "relaxed" and "dynamic". His examples help students break complex concepts into simple ones, as they develop the confidence and skills needed to fully take advantage of their training.

Training Background

- Started training in 1975 while stationed with the U.S. Navy and member of the Naval Security Group on Okinawa. He was privileged to spend many hours working out directly under 10th degree Okinawan Shorin-Ryu Matsumura Seito Karate and Kobudo Grand Master Fusei Kise in the honbu (home) dojo in Okinawa City. Sensei Gravelle was lucky enough to meet and test under Grand Master Hohan Soken.
- Very privileged to attend training sessions with Grand Master Hohan Soken, founder of Shorin-Ryu Matsumura Seito Karate and Kobudo.
- Attended many karate camps when Master Kise and Kaicho Isao Kise have visited the United States and has visited Okinawa many times in the past years to train personally with Master Kise and Kaicho Isao Kise.
- Trained on Okinawa with 8th Degree Black Belt Ed Gingras.
- Trained with Sensei Kirk Jaeger and Shihan Barry Holck in Shorin-Ryu Kobayashi Karate and Danzan-Ryu Jujitsu.
- Trained with 8th Degree Black Belt Hanshi John Shipes.

- Trained with 8th Degree Black Belt Hanshi Juan Carlos Jöcker.
- Attended Seminars with 8th Degree Black Belt Hanshi Greg Lazarus.
- Attended seminars with 8th Degree Black Belt Hanshi Jeff Ader.

Certifications

- Kyoshi Certificate
- 7th Degree Black Belt Shorin-Ryu Matsumura Seito Karate and Kobudo.
- 7th Dan Instructor Certificate
- OSMKKF U.S. Northwest Regional Manager
- Sensei (Instructor) for Karate, empty hand self-defense.
- Sensei (Instructor) for tuite, joint locks.
- Sensei (Instructor) for kobudo, weapons.
- International Law Enforcement Certificate
- Member of All Okinawa Shorin-ryu Karate & Kobudo Federation (AOSKKF).
- Member of Okinawa Shorin-ryu Matsumura Karate & Kobudo Federation (OSMKKF).
- Shiatsu

Teaching Background

- Founder and Shihan (Head Instructor) for Northwest Budokan - Master Kise's Pacific Northwest Dojo.
- Shihan (Head Instructor) for the Snohomish County YMCA Adult and Youth Karate programs.
- Founder and Sensei (Instructor) for Master Kise's Chandler, AZ Dojo.
- Instructor with "The Young Olympians" in Arizona sponsored by the Boys and Girls Clubs in the Phoenix area.
- Instructor for women's Self Defense seminars.
- Preformed many self-defense demonstrations for community awareness.

Jay Gravelle is available for seminars and speaking engagements.

Master Kise and Sensei Jay Gravelle
at Honbu Dojo in Okinawa

Sensei Jay Gravelle Receiving
Kyoshi Certificate from Kaicho

Contact Information

NorthWest Budokan
Master Kise's Pacific Northwest Dojo
3631 Federal Ave.
Everett, WA 98201
425-783-0884

Shihan@nwbudokan.com

www.NWBudokan.com

11954235R00079

Printed in Great Britain
by Amazon.co.uk, Ltd.,
Marston Gate.